Chats with
My Three Olivias

OTHER BOOKS BY MARIAN OLIVIA HEATH GRIFFIN

CULTURAL GUMBO: OUR ROOTS, OUR STORIES

A DIARY OF LETTIE'S DAUGHTER

THEN THERE WAS NIA

BORN IN A SHACK DID NOT HOLD
ME BACK MAMA FANNIE

Chats with
My Three Olivias

Marian Olivia Heath Griffin

Library of Congress Control Number: 2019904458
ISBN: Hardcover   978-1-7960-2823-2
                 Softcover   978-1-7960-2821-8
                 eBook   978-1-7960-2822-5

Print information available on the last page.

Rev. date: 04/16/2019

To order additional copies of this book, contact:
Xlibris
1-888-795-4274
www.Xlibris.com
Orders@Xlibris.com
795600

CONTENTS

Author's Notes..vii
Acknowledgments xiii
Introduction...xvii

Chapter I   Are You Coming Over? 1
Chapter II   Days Gone By 3
Chapter III   We're Here 6
Chapter IV   Let The Games Begin 10
Chapter V   Grandma G Was First 13
Chapter VI   Harry's First Day..22
Chapter VII   Dinner Time 26
Chapter VIII   Olivia Christina's Brainteasers 29
Chapter IX   Victoria Olivia's Turn 32
Chapter X   Michael Gerard Ii (Lil Mike's) First Day 34
Chapter XI   Amelia Grai's Special Birthday Party....................46
Chapter XII   Sophia Morgan – New Sheriff In Town.................49
Chapter XIII   First Snowfall 51
Chapter XIV   Next Day's Adventure 53
Chapter XV   Christian-Paris' Eagle Scout Celebration 58
Chapter XVI   Grandpa Bert Speaks 64
Chapter XVII   Kiara's Expressions – High School Graduation 68
Chapter XVIII   The Halloween Mini Bus 73
Chapter XIX   Ripley's Haunted House Adventure....................76
Chapter XX   Nia Olivia's First College Day 83

Conclusion 89
Bibliography..93
Reference Books 97
Sources..99

AUTHOR'S NOTES

CHILDREN ARE LITTLE grown-ups. Grown-ups are big kids. So let it be written!

My children and grandchildren have helped me to grow up. When I see some of the things that my children have helped me with and other positive things that my grandchildren do and say, I know there is hope for us in the world.

Our children of today are already writers, architects, great technologists, scientists, teachers and preachers,

One of the greatest joys of being a grandparent is having the opportunity to look forward to the future from another generation's point of view and help them look back to understand their past.

All of humanity is the brushstrokes of God's handiwork. We can only imagine the overwhelmingly beautiful creations that are not only miracles but mysteries from our God.

I have three loving granddaughters who were named after me-Olivia. They are Nia Olivia, Victoria Olivia and Olivia Christina. It honors me to have these children named for me.

WHAT'S IN A NAME? BIG STUFF!

Wise is the person who would rather give honor than receive it.

All my other grandchildren, Kiara Janelle, Christian-Paris, Michael Gerard II, Amelia Grai and Sophia Morgan – all Griffins, might as well have been named Olivia because I love them just as much.

Just to let you know, we feel privileged to be in the grandparent league. We try to nurture other children around us. We get invitations to all sorts of events; grandparent day at two or more schools, sports, high school musicals, marching band parades, choir concerts, violin and piano recitals, Halloween parties, dance contests and recitals, kindergarten graduations, high school graduations, just to name a few.

I am writing this book in an effort to show that children have true emotions as well as adults. Expressions of achievement, comprehensive savvy and marvelous perception may be a natural part of a child's life.

Children are very vulnerable and we must work hard to allow them to have a childhood. We as adults hardly ever think of our children as psychological, sociological and physical beings. Sometimes they do not have adequate survival skills and sink into neverland.

We as grandparents get to make up for all the mistakes we made with our children by helping to raise our grandchildren and other people's children. We get to be gentler with grandchildren. "Gentleness is a term that suggests a kind and gracious soul."

The New Testament has a word for the virtue that corrects our unpleasantness – gentleness. In Ephesians 4: 2, we are reminded to "Be completely humble and gentle."

"Humility toward God will make us gentle toward others."

In other words, we get a second chance. There is often a special bond between grandchildren and grandparents. As a child, I was always happy around my grandparents. My Grandpop Herbert came to our house from the Fountain Homestead, bearing gifts of peppermint candy. I can remember sitting on his lap and reaching my little hand into a brown paper bag and getting a piece or two of that candy. As a little girl, I stuffed that candy into my mouth, looking for more. But the next child was waiting in line to sit on Grandpop Herbert's lap and experience the joy of eating a piece of candy.

Grandpop Herbert also brought us home- made citrus bread. We didn't like the citrus bread because it was never sweet enough. We ate it anyway. I think my siblings and I learned early that adults had feelings too. We did not want to object to anything that our grandfather did for us. He seemed to be as sweet and impressionable as we were.

Then there was Grandmom Hattie who lived in a small town in Accomack County, Virginia. Daddy drove us almost every month from a little town in Delaware to see his mother, Grandmom Hattie. She owned a grocery store, the only one for miles around. Whenever we arrived, there were crowds of people gathered in the store shopping or just standing around to keep warm if it was wintertime.

Grandmom Hattie always wore a long cotton print dress with a long apron over it. I don't remember anyone wearing thick long dresses like that except an old lady that came to our church. She also wore high top boots.

As we came into her store, Grandmom Hattie came from around the counter to grab and hug us. We playfully ran back out of the store so she would run after us in the yard. As she caught us to give her hugs and kisses, we would run back into the store. Everyone was laughing by the time Grandmom Hattie finished this ritual. She was out of breath and everyone else was laughing, including our parents.

Normally Grandmom Hattie was strict and stern. She lectured people constantly throughout the day. When her seven grandchildren came from Delaware to see her, she became ecstatic and playful. All those around her became her playmates.

Grandmom Hattie gathered us and took us back into the store to visit with her or help wait on customers. Lunch time, my sweet grandmom started cutting hunks of cheese from a big round wooden box. A handful of ginger snap cookies or a honey bun went with the sizable piece of cheese for all of us. If other children, especially our cousins were at the store, they received their share of cheese and a honey bun or ginger snap cookies, also.

Some of those children were Daddy's cousin, Grace's children. We loved playing with Joyce and Leonard and especially Martin. I might have been ten when Martin was four years old. Nancy and I remember swinging Martin around and around out in the yard. His mother, Grace and her family lived across the street from Grandmom Hattie's store.

We went across the street to speak to Grace and hold Janet and feed her. Janet was the youngest child at that time, but not for long. Grace was due to have another child any day now.

I think these cousins were all younger than we were except for George Edward, but we enjoyed playing with them when we went to Virginia.

On one of those visits, we came into Grandmom Hattie's store and saw a little cute girl standing around adults.

I said, "Whose little girl is that, Grandmom."

"OH, one of your cousin's children," she answered. "Her name is Sandra."

Changing the subject, Grandmom Hattie said, "I have someone across the way at the house cooking dinner for us. This snack will hold you until we get to the house and eat dinner."

George Edward Heath (named after my Daddy George Wesley Heath) told me much later that he was the one across the way (at the house) cooking dinner. That is why he couldn't come and play with us.

Grandmom Hattie and her sisters, Mary and Annie, were always helping other people to raise their children. I was away in graduate school and was unaware of either of these three dear sweet sisters' deaths and I did not attend either of their funerals.

I was especially saddened by Grandmom Hattie's funeral which I did not know about until afterwards. I was out of state in graduate school during the time of Grandmom Hattie's funeral. I heard from relatives that many people came from near and far to express their sad feelings at the demise of these three ladies.

In fact, my two younger sisters, Hattie Elvira (named for Grandmom Hattie) and Nancy Virginia Heath (named for Mother's aunt, Nancy Harper) told me that there were over a thousand people surrounding the church and lined up in the streets for almost a mile for the funeral of Grandmom Hattie.

She had been the mid-wife for over a thousand children, including all of her grandchildren and nieces and nephews and great nieces and nephews. So many wanted to speak at her funeral.

Some of those parents went to work in the fields and factories. Their children were cared for at Grandmom Hattie's grocery store and Great Aunts Mary and Annie in their homes. These three sisters were mid-wives and had delivered these babies.

This helped us to grow up and have precious times as small children with our families. No one understands this better than I do now. I see children around the world being exploited and abused in a most detestable cruel way that inflicts irreparable harm to the children. It is a national and international issue and catastrophe that so many children, especially minority children are being mistreated with disparities and disrespect before they are old enough to speak for themselves.

Jesus recognized the fact that children need our protection. They need to know that they are worthy of our love and praise and adoration. Children need to be able to reach up and look up to God and trust Him. First, they have to be taught how to pray. They need to know that there is someone who cares deeply for them through support programs.

I used to actually think as a small child that one day I would be just like my Grandpop Herbert and Grandmom Hattie. They were both sensitive to the needs of children. There was a deep and abiding love for each child they met and I wanted to strive for that and be like them.

I have heard it said, "When I grow up, I want to be just like you." If you mean it, write it down as one of your goals in life."

Even though I did not write it down as a goal, I'm still working at that thought and possibility.

ACKNOWLEDGMENTS

I AM PLEASED to acknowledge and thank the persons who have allowed me to use their real names.

I am grateful to my parents, Lettie Harper Heath and George W. Heath, Sr from whom I learned so much. I had great grandparents: Sadie Fountain Harper and Herbert Harper and Hattie Wise Heath and William 'Will' Heath. They helped me share experiences by interacting with my siblings and me. My grandparents encouraged me to choose hope and faith instead of fear and dismay.

I am privileged to have grown up with a large family. I was lucky to have six siblings, three deceased and three living.

They are Phyllis Heath Pepper (deceased), George W. Heath, Jr, Daniel L. Heath, Sr, (deceased) Joseph B. Heath, Sr, Nancy Heath Kellam and Hattie E. Heath Purnell (deceased.)

Our three children, Bertrand Griffin II, Karen Griffin Phenix and Michael Gerard Griffin have always been my pride and joy even when they were young and required so much attention and care.

As adults, they are resourceful in my research for authentic and documentary material.

They are truly good people to talk to especially now that they are adults. Likewise, my children's spouses: Tosha, Keith and Tracie. They are a joy in which we discuss issues and situations.

Keith Phenix, our son-in-law, edits my work. I am so grateful to him for this service. I can rely on him.

Then our eight lovely grandchildren and extended grandchildren are inspirational and insightful. They are always my special little people: Nia Olivia, Kiara Janelle, Christian-Paris, Michael Gerard (Lil Mike), Amelia Grai, Victoria Olivia, Olivia Christina and Sophia Morgan – all Griffins. I have a grand god daughter, Amelia Pleasant and her little brother, Warren Pleasant, whom I adore.

A special thank you to three of our cousins- Janet Nock Moreno, Rose Brown Kelly and Dan Carter for continued family information and stories.

I have been into close contact with some beautiful human beings, many more than I can list here. I am grateful for my friends at St Mark United Methodist church.

To my precious St. Mark United Methodist clergy, Pastor Simon Chigumira, retired ministers: Rev. Bertrand Griffin, Sr., Rev. Glorious Wright, and Rev. Willie Laws and our former pastor – Dr Derrick Hills, thank you for all you do.

My St. Mark United Methodist church family is special to me and I will forever cherish them. Especially my Cherubim Choir, past and present members, the Sanctuary choir, Female Ensemble, Male Jubilee and Youth choir.

Other precious members of the St. Mark family are Lorita Frank, Charlotte Burkhalter, Vinnie Davis, Edwina Jackson, Tracie and Marelyn Branch, Oletha Dees, Terri Sanderford, Dollene Sims, Ethel Blaze, Dorothy Collins, Michelle Thomas, Rozelyn McGee, Melvin and Sylvia Sanders, Melvin and Sandra Sanders, Jr, Catherine and Semmie Martin, James Bowman, Loyd Northern, Earnest Lee, Eunice Simmons and Sophia Ennin.

We formed a NINETY-PLUS group when Eleanor Miles told me she was making her ninety -first birthday about ten years ago and asked me to take her picture. We formed the ninety- first group because Eleanor said there was no one to look out for elderly people in our church. That day I took pictures of Eleanor Miles, Mildred Bowie, Doris Thompson, Eloise Williamson, Mable Jackson, Mary Taylor, Nathlie Holloman, Alice Stepter and Vertlee Washington (who moved from New Orleans after the Katrina Hurricane and flood in 2005.)

We started the special birthday celebration in 2009 and continue to honor and serve these elderly foxy ladies and have added others, such as Emily Marshall, Ruth Myers and Ruth Eby, Ella Pitts, Mary Matthews and Milton Grayer as they became ninety-plus. Eleanor and four others are over one hundred years old. Some have passed on. St. Mark United

Methodist church has changed administrations and pastors but the ninety-plus group still stands.

I organized a Cherubim choir forty-six years ago at St. Mark United Methodist Church, for which I am pianist and director. I am proud of them all, past and present. My Cherubim choir members have grown up to be model citizens and professionals in engineering, medicine, chemistry, teachers, ministers, armed services personnel, social workers, nurses, mental health counselors, writers, deputy sheriff, politicians, business men and women, food service managers, law enforcement offices, truck drivers, corporate leaders and other careers in their respective communities. Ninety five percent of these cherubim choir members graduated from high school and ninety-percent graduated from college. We are so proud of them.

I am grateful to the genealogy staff at the East Baton Rouge Main library on Goodwood Boulevard for all of their assistance in doing my research.

Thanks to the library staff members at the Scotlandville Branch Parish library who have been so helpful: They are Chad Cooper, Jennifer I. Thompson, Pamela A. Donaldson and Charles H. Shropshire.

I am honored to acknowledge many special friends who have been supportive of me over the years: Dr. Leslie and Rozetta Norris, Dr. Jonathan and Geraldine Roberts, Dr. Jesse L. Douglas, Rev. Robert and Helen Williams (deceased) and Dr. George Calvin and May Calvin Belton (deceased.)

Let me thank the members of my Alpha Kappa Alpha sorority for their support: including Janifer Peters, Lorita Frank, Susie Boudreaux, Gwen and Jaimelle Thomas, Gloria and Carmen Spooner, Judy P. Reed, Kismet Gray, Dr. Myrtle Joyner, Melba Moye, Sanettria G.Pleasant,(cousin), Marvis H. Lewis, Sandra Hall, Dr. Katina Semien, Esq.(South Central Reginal Director), Dr. Lovenia-Deconge-Watson, Dr. Beverly Wade (deceased), Geraldine and Joni Roberts, Marilyn Ray Jones, Tamara Montgomery, Dr. Julia Purnell, (deceased), Karen Griffin-Phenix (daughter) and so many others. Gamma Eta Omega chapter of ALPHA KAPPA ALPHA SORORITY continues to make a viable presence in the lives of so many people and in the world.

I am honored to be in the family of so many great people: Sally Gillespie Newman, Brenda Cooks, Edwin Cooks, Diane Cooks, Linda Cooks and Johnnie Narcisse and family, Janet Nock Moreno and family, Martin Anthony Nock and family, Sandra Brickhouse, Bessie Lawrence and family, Rose B. Kelly and family and a whole host of other relatives.

To Elaine Sims and the Beauty Shop Bunch. Thank you. You are so inspiring!

I always save the acknowledgment of my husband, Bertrand Griffin, Sr for last. "The last shall be first, and the first shall be last. What is good and wholesome and successful in my life, I owe to God and my husband.

"The Lord, your God, is in your midst, a warrior who gives victory. He will rejoice over you with gladness,

He will renew in his love; He will exult over you with loud singing. Zephaniah 3: 17, NRSV.)

I SINCERELY LOVE ALL OF YOU.

Historical Perspective

CHILDREN ARE EXPLORERS. They love to discover new things and are very crafty in their discoveries. They are mischievous and cunning. They connect to their world through a child's eyes. They can run an adult up a tree in a heartbeat with their questions and arguments, if they are anything like my children and grandchildren.

This generation of children has had more adventures and more advantages than any generation since the Wild, Wild West Movement! Our grandchildren have attended many events. Concerts, plays, operas, sports, museums and presidential inaugurations are just a daily part of their routine.

Consequently, it has become our regular routine as well. We have to juggle our schedules in order to be a part of our grandchildren's lives and activities.

Their travels are more extensive than other generations. We have taken several trips to Gatlinburg, Tenn. The grandchildren love Disney World Theme parks in Orlando, Fla and adventures in Gatlinburg. They have gone on cruises with the family. This is the positive side of the story.

Their experiences with technology and astronomical experiments are exceptional. What an age and generation we have to look forward to in our children's effort to help save the world.

We must teach them how to live a happy and successful life. "Give them a sense of pride, as the song writer said in THE GREATEST LOVE and help them to value themselves."

Relationships between parents, grandparents and other adults and children can be very complicated, but it doesn't have to be that way. There is evidence that love conquers all ills, struggles and fears.

There should be a fusion between the generations an acknowledgement of accomplishments and successes of the generations especially the children. We as adults have to be 'the adults in the room.'

There is leadership among the children as well as the adults. Communication and accommodation are keys to open doors. We can find strength in our differences. We can celebrate and empower each other.

Whether we are at home, in the work place, at school or in the community, we can make positive strides to impact our diverse lives with pride.

There are programs such as the one with the National Urban League which fosters entrepreneurship in several cities across the nation to assist children and youth in Middle school and high school to get off to a successful start in life.

Our children have dazzling and groundbreaking minds and daring skills They are waiting and wanting to be discovered and recovered from all the ills and struggles in their lives.

Let them proclaim to the world that they are todays leaders as well as tomorrow's leaders. Team up with them and leave it to them to express themselves.

Many are no longer waiting. They are working toward the prize with the help of God working for and through them. All they need is a little encouragement and a lot of prayers in order for them to soar.

"Fredman-Gonzalez noted that by 2011, The National Urban League had impacted the following cities: Atlanta, Chicago, Cincinnati, Cleveland, Houston, Jacksonville, Fla., Kansas City, Mo., Los Angeles, New Orleans and Philadelphia. (www.time.com/adsections.)

Finding help for our children and youth should be one of our major priorities in life. They are not only our future, as many people say. They are our present as well as our past.

Lots of children are dealing with adult situations and problems. They need help to bounce back into a more secure and productive life.

Children can tolerate much but we must recognize the vast differences in each child, even in the same family.

I marvel at the many children's choir members over the years because they came from single mothers' home, yet they are being successful in their lives.

Hebrew 12: 1 urges us to "run with perseverance" and teach our children to do the same."

We must instill in our children good habits and self-assurance that will enhance their ability to survive in the world.

"The word perseverance denotes and fore-warns that the race we are called to run will be challenging with trials and tribulations, and that we would have no need to persevere if that were not true," I said.

Charles E. Blake, Sr. states in his book, FREE TO DREAM, "Never surrender to hopelessness." Never take your eyes off the dream. Keep the dream before you- the dream for yourself and your people. Continually seek God's heart in every matter." (p.15.)

Encourage children and let them know that their God is always with the.

CHAPTER I

Are You Coming Over?

ONE SATURDAY AFTERNOON, our son Michael and his wife, Tracie dropped in on us with their five children. We didn't have any plans for the day, so we were just relaxing. I knew it was Grandpa Bert's eighty-fourth birthday. I also knew that our children were coming over from their respective cities in Louisiana to be with their loving father on his eighty-fourth birthday.

They had each planned to come over and see their father on his birthday but did not want him to know it. Neither of our children called us that week for fear of spilling the beans.

Normally we had conversations with our children almost daily which was a joy. Not so much this week.

At the last minute, Saturday morning, Michael called and said, "What you-all doing?"

"Nothing," I replied. "Just hanging out."

This is our usual conversation in the morning- very cordial and noncommittal.

"I was thinking about coming over a little later, maybe around noon when the kids and Tracie get up and get ready. They are still sound asleep. They stayed up late and played a new dance game with music from the TV last night. And Lil Mike is still in Summer school until next Wednesday so he was studying."

"Karen and Keith and Bertrand and Tosha might be on their way over, too. Don't worry about cooking anything. We'll bring a bite to eat. And we will set up two card tables in the den when we get there. Don't give Dad his birthday card or anything yet."

"And don't stress yourself out. The children will just dirty the house up again. You know, they are just children."

Bertrand II and Tosha lived in Kenner. Karen, Keith and Christian-Paris lived in Monroe. Michael, his wife Tracie and their five children lived in New Orleans. They all moved back to Louisiana when they started having children and raising them.

Once upon a time, I thought my three children would never get along with each other. They were always competing with each other. We were trying to raise them right in the sight of God.

"Boy was it a pain!"

Grandpa Bert was always telling them, "you are all Griffins, well Heath/Griffins because you got half of your mama in you, too. What's in a name? You don't know the half of it."   "Heath,   that's   your mother's last name. It means a 'tree' planted by the water. "She shall not be moved, and she is stubborn as a mule," Grandpa Bert told them.

"Griffin means half eagle, half lion, king of the beast and king of the birds of the air, with a short bob-tail."

The short bob-tail always made the children laugh.

CHAPTER II

Days Gone By

WHEN OUR THREE children, Bertrand, II, Karen and Michael were young and in elementary school, I drove them to school every day. They would fuss and fight over the two back windows each morning. One day, I decided to let the oldest child, Bertrand II, sit in the front seat with me on the passenger's side and the other two children had a window, one left and one right on the back seat.

This worked fine until the two younger children complained that they wanted to sit on the front seat sometimes. They could see better in the front. Incidentally, this was before seat-belts and children's car seats.

OK! Another plan was called for. I wouldn't have any peace in the car until we worked something else out.

I said, "each child will have his or her turn to sit in the front seat for a week, but that child will wash dishes and clean up the kitchen every day that week. Agreed?"

"I cook breakfast and dinner each day and one of you clean up the kitchen every day. Oh, and by the way, each of us will make up his or her own bed as soon as you get out of it. Agreed?"

"Agreed," my children all chimed simultaneously.

"But what about Dad?" asked five years old Michael. "Who's going to cook for him and make up his bed?"

"Mike, don't sweat the small stuff. I got that covered," I said.

"Your Daddy goes to work at five o'clock every week-day morning and seven o'clock on Sunday morning. He's a chaplain and works out of town. So, his schedule is special and separate from ours. He has to drive sixty miles one way to the Angola State Prison, that's one hundred-twenty miles daily. He's tired when he gets home."

"We got our schedules straight when Michael was in first grade, Karen was in second grade and Bertrand II was in fifth grade. One down and much more to go!"

With small children, there is always something to argue about. They were constantly telling on each other.

I woke up one morning thinking, "Children are little adults and grown-ups are big children. You have to treat them that way and train them."

That day I told our children, "when each of you become adults, I want each of you to find your own state to live in and don't let it be Louisiana."

After college and graduate school, each of our children found their own state. Bertrand II chose the state of Washington to work in chemical engineering and get his Masters degree in management after attending Dillard University and receiving his bachelor degree.

Bertrand II received the call to preach later and left Washington to attend Gammon Theological Seminary in Atlanta, Georgia. He and his family lived there until he completed his Masters degree in Theology. Then he returned to Louisiana and started his ministry in the local church.

Karen completed her bachelor degree at Xavier University and Masters degree at Southern University. She also attended S.U. Law School for one- and one-half years. She selected Houston and worked there for sixteen years in Mental Health Counseling before returning to Louisiana with her family to work in the same field.

Michael attended Dillard University at the age of seventeen and went into the United States Army around the same time after high school. He was called to active duty and sent to Desert Storm in the Middle East to fight in the war around 1991 after he completed one semester at Dillard.

Michael returned to the States, went back to Dillard University and completed that degree in Health Care Administration. He entered MeHarry Medical College, received a Masters degree in his chosen medical field. After completing his externship at a clinical setting in

Evansville, Indiana, he secured a job in Austin, Texas with his new wife for two years.

After that job, Michael moved to Birmingham, Alabama and enjoyed working at a medical facility in Jefferson County, then at the University of Alabama in Birmingham. He built (remodeled a one -hundred- year old home) in Birmingham and started two businesses in Birmingham.

Two babies later, Michael and his wife, Tracie returned to New Orleans, Louisiana. He is currently working in his field as President/ CEO as health care administrator for the Daughters of Charity.

Each of our children went away from home, got a taste of the world and then returned to Louisiana – with families.

"Fantastic!"

CHAPTER III

We're Here

AS THE GRANDCHILDREN, Nia Olivia, Kiara Janelle, Christian-Paris, Michael II, (Lil Mike), Amelia Grai, Victoria Olivia, Olivia Christina and Sophia Morgan were coming into our home for Grandpa Bert's birthday party, there was much happy greetings, hugs and kisses.

The parents and older grandchildren were bringing in tons of food, two birthday cakes, gumbo, fish and chicken, so many types of side dishes: salads, casseroles, collard greens and oyster dressing.

Each of our children brought their specialty. Karen had a large potato and sausage casserole which is always our favorite. Keith had a carrot, raisin and pecan cake and his sister's cornbread dressing.

Michael had several large containers of fried fish, crabs and crawfish, the collard greens, baked beans and peas. Tracie loves to make salads. She brought in a fruit salad and a lettuce, tomato and cucumber salad. Amelia Grai made an apple pie.

Bertrand II and Tosha came in with several sweet potato pies, pecan pies and ice cream.

The parents began setting up tables and trays for the whole family in our spacious den.

The biggest surprise for Grandpa Bert was Aunt Nancy and Uncle Albert sauntering in off the twenty- two hour drive from Delaware. Grandpa Bert was so happy he just reared back in his rocking chair and closed his eyes.

"I made another big birthday, you guys! Thank you so much for remembering me."

Sophia Morgan gave us another surprise by running up to Grandpa Bert, climbing on his lap and hugging him. They sat there and rocked each other.

"You're the oldest and I am the youngest Griffin."

Sophia started singing, "It's so nice to be with Jesus, isn't it nice."

I don't think Grandpa Bert had ever heard that song before, but he started singing it with Sophia.

Both Michael and Tracie, her parents, were shocked because they had not told Sophia that piece of BREAKING NEWS.

Her older siblings had not mentioned that fact either: that Grandpa Bert was the oldest and Sophia was the youngest Griffin.

"That is very discerning of you, Sophia, to know that you are the youngest Griffin and Grandpa Bert is the oldest Griffin," I said.

"I know," said Sophia. "That just came to my brain. Grandpa Bert is Jesus."

Every one cracked up laughing.

"Well, I'm not Jesus, but I try to be like him."

"But you are Jesus," Sophia insisted. "I have seen pictures of Jesus and I have seen pictures of you." She hugged Grandpa really tight then climbed down from his lap.

At that moment the doorbell rang and other family members were coming in, bearing gifts and food. Francine, Linda, Aggie and Whitney Cannon, our nieces came with several flavors of ice cream, another cake and gifts.

Sanettria, her husband, Gregory and their children, Amelia and Warren Pleasant were peeping their heads in the door. They are Grandpa Bert's cousins.

"Are we late?" asked Sanettria. "I thought the party started at two o' clock."

"It does," said Aunt Karen; "but we all had to get here from out of town. That's why we said that everyone should be here by two o'clock."

The greetings and hugs and kisses started all over again.

Little Warren handed Grandpa Bert a bouquet of yellow roses and Amelia gave him a handwrapped gift.

Grandpa Bert was very happy.

Have you-all sung 'Happy Birthday' to Cousin Griffin, yet? I would start it, but I can't sing," said Sanettria.

"I repeated an old saying that a lady, Yvonne McDomic, told me in church one day."

She said, "Everyone can sing, but a buzzard."

Nia Olivia said, "Grandma G, you are so funny. I can't believe some of the saying you come up with."

The whole room was laughing.

"I don't always come up with these sayings, Nia Olivia. I just write them."

"Let me tell you children how our latest guests are related to you. Francine, Linda, Aggie and Whitney are my nieces, my brother Daniel's children from Delaware. That's where I am from."

"We already knew Sanettria Glasper and Gregory Pleasant before they got married and before their children were born. During my research into genealogy, I learned that Sanettria's mother's maiden name was Sanders. Grandpa Bert's grandmother's maiden name was Sally Sanders. Sally married Great Grandfather Allen Sam McCullen Gillespie. Years later, the Gillespie family changed their name to Glasper. Sanettria's father was a Glasper.

I have a genealogy chart in my first book, CULTURAL GUMBO: OUR ROOTS, OUT STORIES. The genealogy chart shows the linkage of the Gillespie/Glasper family group. A 1900 United States Federal Census Report indicated that there was a third spelling of this name- Glassby." First Glassby, second Gillespie and third, Glasper. The Glassby/Gillespie/Glaspers all have the same ancestors.

In this room we are all related and Grandpa Bert is the patriarch of the family.

"What does patriarch mean?" asked Victoria Olivia.

"I want to know, too," said Amelia Grai.

"OK, Lil Mike. Dictionary time."

"The dictionary is on the computer desk."

Lil Mike came back into the playroom reading.

"Patriarch means the male ruler, the head of the family, ancestor or chief."

"WOW, all that?" said Olivia Christina.

"Well, Sophia called Grandpa Bert, 'Jesus' earlier. Grandpa denied it but he is over us all on earth. I'm glad," said Christian -Paris. I love my grandpa."

"Me too, he's our chief," the children said simultaneously.

The children were whipping up another song about a chief.

The doorbell rang. Sally Gillespie Newman and her two daughters, Brenda and Linda and Linda's husband, Johnnie Narcisse were coming into the den.

"Sally is Grandpa Bert's first cousin. We are all close kin."

"Sally Sanders was Bert Griffin and Sally Gillespie Newman's grandmother. I know you don't possibly understand these relationships now but you will one day when you get to know your relatives."

I continued, "With incredible courage, these amazing older relatives and their parents and grandparents have weathered the storm, made sacrifices and coped with crucial times so that we can have a secure and happy life."

Sally said, "I'm going to sit right here beside your Granddaddy Bert. I believe that we are the two oldest persons in the room. Today is a good day. We're all getting older and it surely beats the alternative."

"We need you young children around us and you need us around you," said Sally.

CHAPTER IV

Let The Games Begin

WHILE THE BIG people were setting up the tables and situating the family for the fabulous meal, Olivia Christina, our game maker said, "Grandma G, can we play a game?"

"What kind of game do you want to play, Olivia," I asked.

"I don't know. You go first. Your turn to make up a game, Grandma G," she said.

"OK, this is a little game I want to play with you called "First Days.""

"It's a game where you remember something that first happened to you, the first day it happened to you."

"OH, I get it, like your first day at school," Victoria Olivia said.

Olivia Christina said, "Grandma G, I'm too little to remember anything. I'm only five years old."

"Olivia Christina, you have had five whole years to remember something that happened to you."

"Think, Think!"

Nia Olivia, our first grandchild, is in college at Brenau University. I felt that she would be the one to stall because she would feel as if she were too old and sophisticated to play children's games.

"I was right."

Nia Olivia said, "Grandma G, I have to study. I have a term paper to write when I return to school. I have already bought some of my new books that I have to read this next semester. I went up to the school to register this week and got some of my assignments. Also, my track team is going to Canada next month so I have to be caught up with my school work."

"Go ahead, Nia Olivia. We understand that you are bogged down with homework," I said.

"But I do want to hear the other kids play the game."

A light bulb came on into my head. I saw Nia Olivia was warming up to the subject.

Nia Olivia said, "Grandma G, you're the oldest. You should remember way back when you first went to school. Why don't you tell us one of your first days?"

"Yah, Grandma G, you go first. Tell us your first day in elementary school. You might forget your first day before you start telling it," said Victoria Olivia.

All the children started laughing. We were in a playful mood.

"You'll be sorry," I said. Let's go in the playroom while the grown folk set up the tables and set out the food."

"My story was a long time ago and I have a long memory. I'll be telling the long version."

"Why don't we get something to eat first, then tell our 'First Day' stories. It's not like I didn't have a first day," I said.

"I was stalling for time, trying to get my thoughts together."

"I'm going to get something to drink," said Olivia Christina.

"Do you want a drink, Grandma G?"

Victoria said, "Grandma G, you can't remember. You're old as dirt."

Nia Olivia said, "Victoria Olivia, don't be rude to Grandma G. She is just trying to entertain us."

Victoria Olivia was giggling as my three Olivia's and the other children were leaving the play room and going into the kitchen to get drinks.

I thought, "This is out and out grandma- grandchildren war. I may have started something I can't finish."

"OK! Ladies and Gents," I said.

"Sit down because I'm about to tell you a story that will knock your socks off. All three of you Olivia Griffins and the rest of the Griffin grandchildren, pay attention. And we have Amelia P and Warren with us, too.

So, we have three Olivia's- Nia Olivia, Victoria Olivia and Olivia Christina. Now we have two Amelia's- Amelia Grai and Amelia P."

So, the rest of you guys fall in line because you are singles. That means Kiara Janelle, Christian Paris, Michael Gerard II (Lil Mike), Sophia Morgan and Warren Pleasant. I have ten of the most brilliant children in the world sitting in front of me.

"Upps, make that thirteen children! Another family from our church peeped their heads in the door and said, "Can we come in?"

"We heard so much laughter and singing, I know you could not hear the doorbell ring."

"I heard Mrs. Griffin announce that Rev. Griffin was celebrating his eighty-fourth birthday today and we wanted to come by and sing Happy Birthday. This was the Mandy Avila family. We had Justin, Veronica and Miranda."

"Where are Brianna and Lillie?" I asked Miss Mandy.

"OH, they are visiting Brianna's god-mother," answered Miss Mandy.

"We went around the corner from your house and picked up the other Brianna and her little sister, Mya Bates. We just came to sing 'Happy Birthday.'

These children are some of my cherubim choir and we pick them up and carry them to church with us. They feel like they are my grandchildren. And I know they can sing because I have taught them to sing.

Come on in and grab a seat; we're just getting started.

"OH, no, Mrs. Griffin. We're not going to stay. We just wanted to come by in honor of Rev. Griffin and bring him this pineapple up-side-down cake and a little gift, a coffee mug."

"You are so sweet. Please get something to eat and let your children get something to eat."

As the two church families were leaving, Victoria Olivia tugged at my sleeve and said, "Grandma G, it's time for you to tell your first-time story."

CHAPTER V

Grandma G Was First

"I WILL TELL YOU about my first day in elementary school."
"It was almost three quarters of a century ago." I began.

"Three quarters of a century ago! That's almost one hundred years ago," Amelia Grai said.

"Yes, and I was a child like all eight of you and the two Pleasant children are now. I am in my seventies."

"I don't know anyone as old as you are, Grandma G," said Olivia Christina.

"Olivia Christina, Grandpa Bert is older than I am. We are celebrating his birthday today. He is in his eighties."

When I was five years old like you are now, I went to a little two room school in a small town in Delaware."

"Two weeks after I started to school, I had my sixth birthday. My mother Lettie walked me to school holding my hand that first day."

"My two older siblings, Phyllis and George, Jr. were walking ahead of my mother and me with their friends. They were chatting and gigging, just happy to see each other at school again."

"It seemed that each year my parents walked the newest child to school. Entering school was a big day for our family. My Grandmother Sadie watched over the younger children at home while Mother walked me to school."

We walked to the little brown school house. Somehow, I knew that this was a special moment for me and my whole family. This was my first day at elementary school.

As we walked along, I saw several of my young friends who were my age. They were walking with their mothers and fathers. They would be in my class.

"Some of my classmates were Margaret, Geraldine, Leroy and Leslie (the twins), Abraham and Jonah. There were four children that I did not know. I knew all the children and the teacher's names except for the four new tall children. As we walked up the steps to the school, our teacher, Miss Daniels met us at the door. Our parents came to register us in school."

Olivia Christina and Victoria Olivia said simultaneously, "Our Mother and Daddy went to school with us, too. They drive us to school every day, but the first day, they went inside with us."

"Yes, I remember seeing your first day school picture, Olivia Christina," I said.

Victoria Olivia continued, "Sophia is going to kindergarten school next year. She is the youngest, so Mommie and Daddy will drive her to school, too.

"Well, I guess the 'first day' ritual is a tradition in this family."

"When I saw your 'first day' school picture, Olivia Christina, I noticed that you looked a little frightened," I said.

"That's why I wanted to hear about your first day," I said.

Olivia Christina said, "I was scared. Mom walked out of the classroom and I followed her. She turned around and took a picture of me on the steps. I laugh at that picture now."

"Your Grandpa Bert and I drove each of our children, Bertrand II, Karen and your Daddy Mike G to school and walked them inside on their first day," I said.

"This was our way of encouraging them and helping them to get adjusted to their first year at school."

Victoria Olivia said, "Grandma G, what did you do on your first day?"

"When our parents left, we started playing. Many of these children were already my friends from church and our neighborhood. Miss Daniels asked us all to sit down. After we sat down, she asked us one by one to stand and state our names."

My turn came. I proudly stood up and said, "My name is Marian Olivia Heath." The children giggled because I said my whole name. My mother had taught me to be proud of my name and be proud of who named me. That is why I am so proud to have three grandchildren named Olivia after me."

The other children that I knew stated their names – Margaret Smith, Geraldine Hobbs, Leroy and Leslie Benson, Abraham Sanders and Jonah Hanson.

Then a big boy who was bigger than my older brother, George, stood up and said his name was Harry.

The teacher tried to get Harry to say his last name.

Olivia Christina said, "Harry did not know his last name."

"You are absolutely right, Olivia Christina. Harry could not tell us his last name and started crying."

"Miss Daniels went to her desk and jotted down a note. Then she handed Harry a tissue to blow his nose. Harry and his older sister, Clara had come to school on the bus. They did not have a parent to come and register them.

"There were two other children who rode on the bus from out in the country. Their names were Jackie and Jeanie. They were brother and sister. Jackie, a big boy was cripple. He limped badly on one leg."

"Jeanie was little. She was very pretty. She was six years old but she was smaller than I was. A few weeks after school started that year, Jeanie died. She had some sort of rare condition and she did not survive."

"My first-grade class went to Jeanie's funeral. It was at her house out on the porch. She was lying in a tiny casket and she had on a pink dress. We filed around the casket and then got back on the bus. Then a group of grown-ups gathered around the casket in chairs out on the porch and in the back yard.

"We left on the school bus, but we could hear the people singing."

"Grandma G, what else happened that first day?" prompted Lil Mike.

"After all the children said their names, the teacher assigned us seats. She gave Leslie seat number one. I was given seat number two. Leroy had number three. I was between the two twins. Miss Daniels knew that the twins' mother and my mother were best friends. Placing us together was possibly a way to help us adjust to school.

Harry was placed in seat number four and Margaret drew seat number five. Each child received their respective seat assignments. There were fourteen of us in first grade.

"Harry and Clara, brother and sister, and Jackie and Jeanie, brother and sister were the only four children that we did not know. Harry was ten years old and had never attended school. Clara was eleven years old and had attended first and second grades in another state.

Jackie was ten also. He had attended school only one year. He started late due to his health condition. Jeanie was almost seven years old and had never attended school. Jackie and Jeanie's mother was a migrant worker, also. They did not have a father living with them, we found out later.

"Grandma G, you remember all your classmate's names from first grade," said Kiara.

"I knew most of the children's names, all but the children who rode on the bus. Their parents and grandparents had moved about five miles out in the country and the children had to ride the bus to school. Also, their families did not have cars. These two families had come from Florida to pick crops and had gotten stranded because their truck had broken down in Delaware. They settled there and secured housing."

"Harry and Clara's grandmother, Mrs. Harrington had started walking to our church on Sunday, bringing Clara or one of the older boys with her. Come rain or come shine, snow or sleet, Mrs. Harrington came to church."

That is how my Daddy found out about Harry and Clara, who were brother and sister. Their last name was Taylor. Daddy told Mrs. Harrington that her grandchildren had to attend school and he would request that the bus driver pick up her grandchildren every day. When Daddy learned that there were other minor children in the household, he encouraged Mrs. Harrington to bring them to church every Sunday and let them enroll and come to school every day."

Daddy was Sunday school superintendent at our small AME church. He sought children and encouraged them to attend church all the time. Harry did not come to church with his grandmother. He wanted to stay home with his father all the time.

By the time Harry was required to attend school, he was ten years old, weighed about one hundred forty pounds and was big for his age. He was larger than my older brother, George. Harry should have been in fourth grade with my brother. Yet, he was in first grade.

"Clara was OK, but everything went downhill for Harry."

Olivia Christina cried, "Harry was ten years old, big and didn't know his last name. I knew my first, middle and last name by the time I was two years old."

"That's why names are so important to me, first names and last names. Your name denotes who you are and who you are related to," I said.

"What's in a name? Names were important to my mother. She named her children very carefully. Our names were given to us because of someone special to my mother and father."

"I think it's significant and never to be overlooked, that God named himself. That's another long story," I said.

"Wow, how did God name himself?" asked Amelia- Grai and Amelia P simultaneously, who were sitting together.

"I will tell you later, because it requires more studying on my part. It's a long story, but God has always been here, so he says "I Am who I Am." I said.

"Let me finish about Harry first. He did not really have anyone to teach him things like your mother and father do."

Harry worked alongside of his mother and father and siblings in the fields picking beans and tomatoes. They were more concerned about how much their basket of beans weighted and how many baskets of tomatoes they could pick.

"Grandma G, what's siblings?" inquisitive Victoria Olivia asked.

I knew that question was coming.

"Siblings means your brothers and your sisters," I said.

On the first day of school, Harry received the nickname, 'Black Harry.' He was very dark, very big and very smelly. And besides, he had nappy uncombed hair. He seemed to be afraid of us and rightly so."

"Grandma G, what was wrong with Harry Taylor?" asked Olivia Christina.

"My dear grandchildren, we all had a great first day at school, all except Harry Taylor."

"Harry Taylor did not know his last name, he could not recite his ABC's and he did not know how to tie his shoes."

When our teacher asked us what we had done all Summer, we described that we had a fun time all Summer. We had played and helped around the house."

"Harry and Clara described their Summer as "Picking beans and apples all Summer."

They had come from another state.

"Harry had never seen the inside of a school, nor did he want to go to school. He stayed around the house and helped his father who was cripple," I told the children.

I learned this tidbit after Harry was required to attend school.

"Grandma G, you remember all these things about Harry and all from first grade?"

said Lil Mike.

Christian- Paris reflected, "I went to school from the first through third grade in Houston. That wasn't so long ago. I don't remember all the kid's names, only a few."

"Those were the few children who made an impact on your life, Christian-Paris," I said.

"Clara and Harry made a great impact on my life," I mused.

"Clara had completed two grades of elementary school in another state. They were migrant workers."

But instead of moving on to the next crop season, they had settled in an old shack on the outskirts of our small town. These children were five and six years older than we were."

"They lived out in the country and didn't know many children except other migrant children who came from North Carolina, South Carolina and Florida to pick crops and move on to the next crop area with their parents."

Nia Olivia said, "Grandma G, they had to work like grown-ups and didn't have any time to play."

"That's right," I said. "We still have migrant workers today."

MARIAN OLIVIA HEATH GRIFFFIN

"Because we were young children, we didn't understand nor did we care about their pitiful background. Their families had moved from a fruit farm in Florida on a migrant truck. We learned that the truck had broken down last year."

"Some of the migrant families did not go back to Florida. They found sub-standard housing in our town and other nearby towns in Delaware. When the old truck could not take them to the next crop town, they stayed on the country side of Greenwood."

"Whose house did they live in?" asked Victoria Olivia.

"Mr. Townhouse rented an old shack to the Taylor family for the Winter. They just barely made it through the cold weather because they were used to sunny Florida. There were nine family members in that cabin."

"My daddy met Mrs. Taylor and Mrs. Harrington in the woods when they were breaking holly branches. They were getting ready to make holly wreaths for Christmas and try to sell them."

"Daddy was cutting down a tree for Christmas for our house. He told them they could drop the holly wreaths off at our grocery store/restaurant and he would sell them and give them the money. They did."

"Daddy also invited the family to attend our little AME church."

"Did they come to church," asked Kiara. She seemed very quiet today, kind of in a fog.

"Yes, Mrs. Harrington, the grandmother and Clara walked to church. We took them home."

Daddy told the mother that she had to enroll her children in elementary school.

Daddy told Mrs. Taylor, the children's mother, that her children had to begin school as soon as possible or they would be reported to the school board.

Mrs. Taylor stated that her children did not have clothes to go to school. The children were also running barefooted.

"Mother and Daddy remedied that situation by collecting clothes and food for this family. I learned that whites and blacks gave 'hand-me down" clothes and pieces of furniture to other families in need. My brothers and sisters and I wore some of the finest "hand-me-down" clothes collected by our grandparents and parents. Whenever we complained about used items coming into our house, Mother said, "If you can't use it, give it to someone else. We gave items to other people."

My parents had a restaurant and allowed Mr. and Mrs. Taylor to come in and get food on credit knowing that she could not ever pay for it."

"Grandma G, did you know all of this when you started to school?"

"Yes, we knew about the family's plight, but we had never seen the young children before the first day of school," I said.

"The grandmother walked to church with a long gray dress on every Sunday. She wore an old gray felt hat to match. Her hair was never straightened or neat. She just had that old hat pulled down over her hair. She stood up and gave her testimony every Sunday, just like the other adults."

"My God, I love you and I love all God's children. If I can't do you no good, I 'haint gonna do you no harm," Mrs. Harrington said.

We laughed at her.

Mrs. Harrington's husband had been in World War II. He was injured and had one leg. We heard that he was lucky to be alive. When he left the service, he was homeless for a while. He was ashamed of his peg leg. He finally got back home to his wife, adult children and grandchildren. He never came to church, but he came to our restaurant once and awhile to eat.

"We were children and we thought Mrs. Harrington was so funny. We laughed every time she talked in church."

"My mother was sitting at the piano in church and saw my siblings and me laughing right along with the other children. She was the church musician and could see everything that went on in that church."

"After Mother saw us laughing at Mrs. Harrington, she made us all sit on the front pew and be quiet."

So, all the children sat on the front pew after that incident when Mother caught us laughing and giggling. She knew what we were laughing about."

That's when she decided to organize a children's choir and get a director to sit with us. We wore white tops and shirts and mother's friend Mrs. Olivia Haynes made black skirts and pants for us. We were the only children's choir for miles around. We got invitations to sing at other churches almost every Sunday after our church service.

By the time I was twelve, Mother became ill and turned the children's choir over to me and my elementary school teacher, Miss Daniels. Mother had been teaching me piano since I was two years old sitting on her lap and touching the piano keys. I had an outside piano teacher for only six months.

When my older sister wanted to take piano lessons from another teacher, Mother started teaching me again. These were joyful times for both of us. We bonded and became true mother and daughter. We would walk out in the evening together and go to the beauty shop together. When I was able to drive and had my license, I drove Mother everywhere she needed to go.

We had a close relationship. It was all about the names, our relationship and my mother's dreams for me. I was named for her two best friends and she knew that I loved and respected that.

CHAPTER VI

Harry's First Day

"ONE MORE THING that happened my first day of school was that we teased Harry during the recess period. We went out to play. Harry came down the steps and was walking beside us."

"Some of the children started calling him names. He ran away from us. There was a large field behind our school. We ran Harry out into the field. He fell down. The children gathered around him and called him 'Black Harry', and 'cry baby'. He had a rip in his pants."

The children started a sing-song: "I see your hinney, all black and shiny."

"Then Margaret and I told the other children to leave him alone."

"We did not know how destitute and lonely Harry and his family was. I only knew a little about struggles and suffering. Harry and Clara only came to school because it was mandatory and the state school board demanded that the parents had to send their children to school by a certain age."

Victoria Olivia said, "I've been going to school all my life. I like school."

Olivia Christina stated, "Me, too."

"We get to play and learn and have friends and eat good food."

Nia Olivia said, "we don't always know how other children feel and we have never had hard times in school. Our parents are taking very good care of us."

"Yes, and that was a different time in life that Harry and Clara were living in. It was right after the World War II and the whole United States was suffering."

"Where was Clara when you -all were teasing Harry?" asked Kiara.

"Clara was in another classroom. Her class did not come out to recess with the first graders."

"He didn't have any defense. Harry chose me to be his mentor. Teary-eyed," he said, "Stop running me. Don't run me anymore. I'm tired."

Margaret and I helped Harry to stand up and walked him back into the school to the teacher.

Miss Daniels could see that he was traumatized. We did not tell what happened. Miss Daniels took Harry into the small bathroom and gave him a bar of soap so that he could wash up.

"By the time recess was over, the children came back in to their seats. Miss Daniels asked us to put our heads down on our desks and rest. She probably had seen us running Harry across the field."

"I felt sad and wanted to cry. I had taken part in taunting my new classmate. I knew that was wrong. He did not treat me or my other classmates poorly."

"I realized almost immediately that I felt a lot of guilt for taking part in teasing and taunting Harry. Today that is called bullying. Don't bully other children."

This devilish game played by small children created stress in me and the others. We never did that again."

Miss Daniels let us raise our heads up. She took out a big book from her desk and began reading to us. The book was called BROTHERS GRIMM.

After the reading session which upped our spirits, it was time to go home from school. We lined up and walked out of the school house and down the steps. Our older brothers and sisters were outside waiting for the first graders to come out. Harry and Clara and the other two bus children had to wait inside for the bus.

Harry stayed at our school for three years and finished third grade. Our class tried to restore some dignity and stability to these two classmates. Harry dropped out at the age of thirteen and remained on the farm picking crops with his parents."

"Clara stayed in the Greenwood elementary school and graduated from eighth grade. The principal let Margaret and me sit near Clara and help her with her school work."

She went on to high school but dropped out before my class graduated from eighth grade and went to high school.

In the Bible, Paul wrote to Timothy. He stressed the importance of maintaining his own spiritual health before helping and serving others. He reminded Timothy of his many responsibilities. There were false teachings to contend with and wrong doctrines to correct. But to discharge his duties well, what was most important was to watch his own life and doctrine closely and persevere in them. He needed to take care of his own relationship with the Lord first before he could attend to others. (Timothy 4: 12-16, NIV.)

George Bloomer, stated in his book, THROW OFF WHAT HOLDS YOU BACK, "God is committed to seeing you through every secret weakness and every temptation. God is not intimidated nor is he shocked by our situations."

Bloomer said "You must understand the power of Christ Jesus to destroy every curse and to stand boldly 'in the liberty by which Christ has made us free.' (Gal. 5:1, NIV.)

And that was my first day in elementary school and all the days after went smoother.

"WHO IS NEXT!

"Me, me," said Olivia Christina. "I'm next."

"My teacher let me play a game the first day of school. Can I play it with you-all?"

"Yes, you may. Right now, your parents are calling us to dinner. What a sumptuous looking meal!"

The younger children had assigned seats at our dinner tables. We all knew from the last family gathering that Sophia Morgan has to sit beside her older brother, Michael II, (Lil Mike). He is her partner. She feels comfortable and secure with her big brother. The other three sisters sit together according to their age: Amelia Grai, Victoria Olivia and Olivia Christina.

Mike G was calling to everyone, especially his smaller children. Warren Pleasant was one of the younger children, so he was placed beside Olivia Christina.

There was a lot of loud chatter from the children as Mike G was calling to them.

CHAPTER VII

Dinner Time

MIKE G SAID loudly, "Come to dinner, G-Five! Come to dinner."

He was calling to his five small children, Michael Gerard II, Amelia Grai, Victoria Olivia, Olivia Christina and the baby, Sophia Morgan. They were coming in from the play -room and scrambling to get to their seats.

"Come and eat everybody."

The bigger grandchildren, Nia Olivia, Kiara Janelle, Christian-Paris and Amelia Pleasant followed.

Their plates were on the tables. Everything looked so good and festive. The tables were decorated with large candles and colorful plates and napkins. Aunt Karen, Uncle Keith and Uncle Greg were bringing in the drinks.

Aunt Tracie and Aunt Sanettria were cutting up their youngest children's food.

Grandpa Bert always said the grace before. Today he asked Uncle Bertrand II to say grace.

Uh-oh! I was not near Bertrand II to make him keep it short. Grandpa Bert always says a long grace and I have to squeeze his hand to let him know that God hears even the shortest prayers and graces.

GOD'S PERFECT PEACE

"Yes, Bertrand II's grace was long, too." He decided to read a prayer poem, then say grace.

GOD'S PERFECT PEACE

On days when I feel shackled, let me not forget I'm free.
That You took my sins and nailed them to the cross of Calvary.

My old ways and bad habits were washed clean the day You died.
Forgive me when I cling to them for that's the sin of pride.

And when I try to run my life instead of trusting Jesus,
for that's not the thing to do.

(Frances Gregory Pasch)

Bertrand II continued.

> "Lord, we thank you this day on this special occasion
> of my father's birthday. We thank You for family and
> friends and all our many blessings. Bless this food that
> it might nourish our bodies and enable us to do Your
> will. In Jesus name, we pray."

"AMEN." Everyone said together.

Mike G said, "While we are still standing, lets serenade Grandpa Bert with Happy Birthday."

We all sang the birthday song loudly and happily.

The children began scrambling to their seats.

"Grandpa Bert, how old are you? Grandma G said you are the oldest person in the room."

"That I am," said Grandpa Bert. I am eighty-four years old today. And I am thankful for every day of my life.

At that moment, you couldn't hear a pin drop except for the forks and knives hitting the plates.

"As my old One hundred and two-year-old friend, Eleanor Miles, used to tell me, "it was so quiet in the den, you could hear a rat pissing on cotton."

"I had told that joke before and it always drew a round of laughter."

"Ma," said Mike G. I was trying to listen to your conversation with the kids. You all dealt with some heavy stuff."

"I was listening, too. I don't remember hearing as much about your first days of elementary school as you shared with your grandchildren," said Aunt Karen.

Keith, our son-in-law, said, "Your mother is much older and wiser now and can share things with her grandchildren that she couldn't or didn't have time to talk to her children about."

"Thanks, Uncle Keith, especially about that remark about my being much older."

Even the little ones laughed.

"Now, I like the idea that I am much wiser because I think I am. As I said earlier, grandparents get a second chance."

"Earlier, we didn't have as much time to deal with the psychological and social aspects of our own children's live. We had to deal more with the physical and the upkeep of our children."

"It is not easy to change the past. In fact, we cannot do it. Only God can change things to make a better future for our younger generations."

MARIAN OLIVIA HEATH GRIFFFIN

CHAPTER VIII

Olivia Christina's Brainteasers

OLIVIA CHRISTINA ATE as much as she wanted. She wanted to play her games and riddles.

"Can I play my riddle game now?" she asked.

"When we finish eating, Olivia. Be patient," said Tracie, her mother.

"I'm finished, Olivia," said Victoria Olivia.

"OK," said Olivia Christina. "Here is the first question. What is as big as you are and yet does not weigh anything?" asked Olivia Christina.

Victoria Olivia said, "Can I take a guess?"

"Is it a picture of you?"

"No, but that is a good guess, Victoria. The answer is 'your shadow'.

"Nia Olivia said, "next riddle, Olivia. Let me see if I can guess it."

"What type of words are these: madam, civic, eye and level?" said Olivia Christina.

"Oh, I know. They are palindromes: they read the same forward and backward."

"Right," said Olivia Christina. "You haven't been peeping off my paper, have you, Nia?"

"No, I already knew that," said Nia Olivia.

"Here's another one. I bet no one can get this one."

"A cowboy rode into town on Friday, stayed three days and rode out again on Friday. How did he do that?"

"Let me take a guess," said Lil Mike.

"He came and left and came back again." Then he left again on Friday."

"You were almost right, Mike. The answer is 'The horse's name was Friday," said Olivia Christina.

Olivia Christina went on, "It is an insect, and the first part of its name is the name of another insect. What is it?

Sophia tried to answer this riddle.

"Is it an ant?" she said.

"That's good thinking, SoSo. But the answer is a beetle. It's two insects' names- a bee and a beetle."

Mike G spoke up. "You guys are doing good. Olivia Christina has some great questions and you-all are trying to answer them. Good game."

"Here's another one," chimed Olivia Christina.

"You can hold it without using your hands or arms. What is it?"

Victoria Olivia mused, 'I can hold my doll in my lap without using my hands."

"I can too," said Olivia Christina. "Just so you know, that's not the right answer."

"The answer is: your breath."

"Another one!" stated Olivia Christina.

"I can run, but I can't walk. I have a mouth, but I can't talk. I have a head, but I can't think. I have a bed, but I can't sleep. Who am I?"

"Nobody knows?" asked Olivia Christina.

"I am a river."

"Olivia, you haven't had your first day time story yet. You distracted us with your riddles.

Olivia Christina said, "That was part of my first day. The teacher let me play my games after the class got started."

"When Mom left, I wanted to go back with her. I was standing there watching her walk away from me. Then she turned around and took a picture of me. That made me smile."

"The teacher came and took me by the hand and walked me inside the school. I saw my cousin/playmate, David, and ran over to him. We hugged. Then the teacher told us all to sit down."

She assigned us seats, then asked us our names and what we had done over the Summer time.

"Just like in the old days," I said. "I guess teachers have to know who are in their classrooms and make a roll."

"The teacher gave us a sheet of paper and asked us write our ABC's on it. We did. I knew my ABC's. Some of the children did not," Olivia Christina said.

The teacher wrote on the black board.

Miss Northern. "That was her name."

"Then she wrote the alphabets on the board. We had to copy what she wrote. Then she talked to us. I don't remember what she said."

"She let us go out of the classroom for a little while to use the bathroom and get a drink of water from the fountain. It was almost lunch time. I could smell the food. I was hungry," said Olivia Christina.

"After lunch, we wrote our numbers. Then I asked if I could play a riddle game. She let me play for a short while. I did three questions. None of the other children knew the answers. Miss Northern said I could play my game again another day."

"I was scared when I first got to school. I saw my cousin, David and ran to him. I was not scared anymore. Some of the other children seemed upset most of the day. That's why I wanted to play a game with the other children."

The rest of the day, I had fun. After we did our class work, the teacher let us play.

CHAPTER IX

Victoria Olivia's Turn

"'TORIA', YOUR TURN!" said Olivia Christina. "I want to hear what you have to say."

Aunt Tracie, Victoria's mother was listening.

"Come on 'Toria'. You told us a while ago that you had a great first day in elementary school."

"I did. I had started taking piano lessons and told the children in class what I had learned on the piano and what I had done that Summer. I also wanted to take violin lessons. Now I take violin lessons at the Music Institute in New Orleans. I love taking piano and violin lessons."

"My first day, I knew my numbers up to one hundred and all my alphabets. I knew how to write my name and my parent's names. I'm smart."

"Teacher said I talk a lot in class. I had cousins in my class and we were sharing secrets."

"I like to play games but I like Sudoku best. Teacher gave some of us Sudoku and some of us Word Search games while the other children were finishing their class assignments."

"I like games a lot but I like to play them with other kids. That's why I make up games and look for them in newspapers and magazines," Olivia Christina said tersely.

Where do you get your love of playing games?" I asked.

"Actually, I don't have a clue where I get it. They just come to me. Anything is possible for me," said Olivia Christina.

I said, "Both of you have creative and imaginative minds and can use your genius and potential to do whatever you want in life. You have gifts and discernment and have accomplished much in your young years."

Let me repeat what Miranda Kerr said in her book, TREASURE YOURSELF. All you need is a hearty dose of determination, a significant measure of focus, a sprinkle of passion and a couple of handfuls of positivity." (p.78.)

"Nothing is ever set in stone, "said Cortez Rainey in his book, FREE YOUR MIND. "Change is everywhere." he said.

Rainey went on to say, "you can always change your situation for the better if it is not working for you by letting go of some of the mean habits that hold you back and develop habits that lift you up." (Para., p. 2.)

"Only our God in heaven can show us who we are and bring complete fulfillment and joy to our lives, "said Charles E Blake in his book. FREE TO DREAM.

"We must not allow anyone but God to assign our roles to us. We must stop letting other people limit our dreams for us and assign our role for us." (p.88.)

"We must continually be receiving divine comfort to walk in Peace, achieve our dreams and help others to achieve theirs in order to walk in the Way. Moreover, we must meditate on the things of God rather than the things on earth." (p. 195.)

"Ma, you preached a sermon just then. I can use every one of those tidbits in my sermon next Sunday," said Bertrand II.

"I'm always telling my congregation some of the things that you and Dad taught us when we were little. I guess I'm just following after Dad and his grandfather and his uncles in going into the ministry."

CHAPTER X

Michael Gerard Ii (Lil Mike's) First Day

"LIL MIKE, YOU are in high school now. You have had many first days. So, you can choose one," said Amelia Grai.

"Ok, I'm going to go for it. My first day is going to be about marching in my high school band."

"My high School band is called the ST. AUGUSTINE MARCHING 100. The first day I got out there on that field with the Purple Knights, my heart was racing. We had practiced for more than a month. That day, everyone was watching us. I knew Mom, Dad, Grandma G, Grandpa Bert, Papa J.V. and all my four sisters, half my cousins and aunts and uncles were looking for me."

"Some of my uncles and older cousins had attended the famous St. Augustine High School, so I knew they would be in the bleachers watching their band come out on the field," said Lil Mike.

"You were absolutely right," said Grandpa Bert. We were so excited. It was at the first home football game for St. AUGUSTINE High School and the crowd was ecstatic. The Purple Knights Marching Band came out of the bleachers like little soldiers, in precision."

"It was spectacular, magnificent! You had your cheering section with four little sisters and the rest of us."

"I saw you turn your head and look up. I know you heard us because we were screaming your name," said Grandpa Bert.

Olivia Christina and Victoria Olivia spotted Lil Mike first. The band had just got out on the field.

The girls started jumping up and down and screaming Lil Mike's name. Lil Mike's parents took up the chorus. The stands were roaring for the first few minutes.

We couldn't hear the band. When the crowd realized that they were missing the sounds from the band, they quietened down and sat quietly to hear the music. The band played very well and marched even better.

Most of the boys were freshmen. Oh, I forgot to mention that St. Augustine is an all-boys high school.

Lil Mike selected this school. He is very proud of his school.

We appreciate his selection and realize that his journey is providing him with an in-depth understanding of the sacrifices being made for his schooling.

Lil Mike is maturing and is looking forward to his sixteenth birthday. He is still playing tennis and has played in many sports programs such as soccer, football, basketball and baseball. Apparently, he has settled on tennis and plays in state and regional tournaments every year. We try to attend as many tennis matches as possible.

His family prays for him frequently. In fact, as Kenny Lean said in, TAKE YOU WHEREVER YOU GO, "we pray for our children and grandchildren before they are born."

"I wholeheartedly agree," I said.

MICHAEL II'S ESSAY SCHOLARSHIP

"Lil Mike, you had another very special day in your sophomore year. Your Daddy sent us pictures and an article about you and two of your classmates receiving a scholarship."

"Oh, Yah!" Lil Mike said excitedly. My two friends and I at the St. Augustine high school received the INAUGURAL ALEX SCHOENBAUM Scholarship for writing essays, "he said.

"According to the Crescent City Sports – Live Pre-games Report, New Orleans' Alex Schoenbaum was an All-American football player. His playing as a line- backer at Ohio State in late 1930's was spectacular, magnificent!"

This information was given by Schoenbaum's daughter who remarked that "her father acted more like a quarterback. Following his days of playing for the Ohio's Buckeyes, Schoenbaum went on to found the Shoneys restaurant chain."

"The school program created by his daughter, New Orleans resident and 1988 graduate of Tulane University, Newcomb College and the Jewish Federation of New Orleans was announced last month."

Eighty students submitted essays to the Jewish Federation of New Orleans who sponsored the essay contest.

"So, impressed by the quality of the essays, the sponsors announced at the St. Augustine Assembly that three Purpose Knights students were awarded scholarships.

Michael Gerard Griffin, II was one of the three students honored at the school as recipients.

"There were eighty of my school mates who wrote an essay and three of us won scholarships from the Jewish Federation of New Orleans which were awarded in January, 2019," said Lil Mike.

"My essay detailed and compared the terrible hate and discrimination that was experienced by two religious' institutions in America recently. These two churches' circumstances were discussed in the news for several months."

"I discussed these two tragic events with my mother and father, Tracie and Michael, Sr and with my great grandmother Leah Chase," said Lil Mike

"My parents reiterated that hate and discrimination is on the rise, and is growing as reflected at every turn."

Great Grandmother Chase offered solutions.

"People are people. Everyone should be treated the same in the sight of God. God did not create us to hate and pass judgement on each other. God made us all in His own image. He made one blood. We divided everything up, but everything belongs to God. The sooner we learn that, the better this world will be."

"You are young, Lil Mike. But you think well. You have been raised to believe that you are a child of God and that all people are 'children of God.'

"I have always said, do unto others as you would have them do unto you."
This scholarship will be awarded annually," Jewish Federation of New Orleans CEO, Armie Flelkow said.

Source: CRESCENT CITY SPORTS – Live Pre-games. New Orleans, Louisiana.

CHAPTER XI

Amelia Grai's Special Birthday Party

VERNICE ARMOUR IN her book, ZERO TO BREAKTHROUGH, states that "Leaders are made, not born. Breakthrough is the ability to innovate and implement creative solutions, using your passion, natural aptitude and interests to accomplish personal ambitions. In this fashion, "you may fulfill your life's purpose." (p. XIII.)

Our granddaughter, Amelia Grai is playful and generous. Her parents, Tracie and Michael, say she is very sensitive. I agree with them.

Although she enjoys playing with other children, playing the piano and violin, she is more interested in working with her mother. They both love to cook and bake. They are fascinated with culinary arts.

In fact, Amelia Grai has a BIRTHDAY BAKE SALE each year on her birthday for charity.

Amelia Grai expressed to me, "As I was studying the Bible and preparing to celebrate my first communion, I had a vision that I should do a charity event every year."

"I have so many clothes and toys that I don't know what to do with them all. I do not need anything else. Some of my friends at school do not have things that I have," Amelia Grai said.

I said, "Amelia Grai, you think much like your mother and father and your great grandmother Chase, as well as your great grandparents, Lettie and George Heath." You get your generosity honest.

I've heard it said many times, "age is nothing but a number; I believe it."

I've also heard it said, "Children often get their traits from grandparents and other ancestors. I believe that too."

This child had a dream at the age of seven to do a good deed for the health services in her community in New Orleans.

This community was ravaged by a major storm, Hurricane Katrina on August 29, 2005.

Amelia Grai was little more than a year-old living in Birmingham, Ala with her family. When she moved to New Orleans to live, she saw the remnants of the hurricane years later.

God's work is done through little children as well as adults.

As Amelia Grai was studying and preparing for her 'First Communion' at her church, she had a vision to do a missionary project right in her own community.

Her eighth birthday was coming soon. She requested that her parents not give her the annual kiddie birthday party. Instead, she wanted to sponsor a 'Birthday Bake Sale for Charity.

Each year on her birthday, this child, who started out at the age of seven years old, has a charity bake sale on her birthday. She is very successful with her project and brings together her extended family and many friends, both children and adults.

She has raised up to a thousand dollars in one day just from selling cakes and cupcakes. They are spread out on the kitchen and dining room tables and on the counter at her home. When we attend this festive occasion, we as adults, have as much fun and laughter as the children.

Amelia Grai's siblings help her. They dress up as chefs and waitresses. It's all in fun and so cute. Her parents help as well, but the children are the show stoppers.

"Someone once said, "It's the thought that counts. Amelia Grai had the thought, expressed the idea and carried it to fruition."

What a fantastic and wonderful experience for this young child!

She is already exhibiting her leadership skills and talents. This has enhanced her self-esteem.

Amelia Grai really draws a crowd every year and donates all her proceeds to charity.

Michele Bollinger and Dao X. Tran, editors of 101 CHANGEMAKERS, stated this concept:

"We believe that young people are routinely underestimated in our society. Far from being apathetic or obsessed with texting and playing video games, they are increasingly engaged in figuring out how to change the world around them."

"In the past few years, we have seen young people organizing for LGBT rights, for the Dream Act, for justice for young black men killed by police, marching against sexism, as well as occupying Wall Street." (p. viii.)

"We hope to inspire more young Changemakers to shape their own histories and to fill future books with their stories." (p. ix.)

"We are so proud of you, Amelia Grai.

The other Amelia Pleasant, who had come into our home with her parents, Sanettria and Gregory, and her little brother, was sitting beside Amelia Grai. They had begun chatting, getting acquainted.

Amelia Grai explained that we were playing a game before and after dinner: first days or events.

Amelia P stated that she would play some other time as her parents were preparing to leave to go out of town. Amelia P is a precious and brilliant child and we will hear much from her later.

CHAPTER XII

Sophia Morgan – New Sheriff In Town

"YOUR TURN, SOPHIA," said Victoria Olivia.

The older children were egging the youngest child in the bunch to express herself. She is normally very talkative.

"Come on, SoSo!" (her family nickname.) Olivia Christina was trying to encourage Sophia.

Sophia was being shy. "I don't have any stories or games to play."

"I have not started to real school, yet."

"Actually, you started to school when you were born, maybe before you were born," said Kiara.

The large extended family that you belong to started praying for you months before you were born.

"Before you were a year old, you started walking and talking. That was a first and second event."

"I was at your house when you started walking. Everyone stood up and cheered and clapped." You clapped too, Sophia," said Nia Olivia.

"Right after you learned to walk, you learned to talk. You've never stopped talking," said Mike G, her dad.

"I found a T-shirt in the Bahamas that Summer that said, "I can't talk, but I have an attitude," I said.

"That pretty-much sums it up. When you get your speed up, do you cut up!"

"You quickly learned how to be the boss of the whole family. Of course, you had a very good teacher, none other than Olivia Christina, your buddy."

Sometimes you two get into it, but basically, you two little ones are on one accord. You are 'battle buddies.'

The older children have to watch out for you two. You can get them into trouble in a heartbeat.

CHAPTER XIII

First Snowfall

"THE FIRST TIME we went to Gatlinburg with you, Grandma G, we saw snow for the first time. Since we live in Louisiana, we don't see any snow. It hardly ever snows in our town," said Lil Mike.

Lil Mike went on to say, "I was sleeping in the den on the sofa bed. I heard a funny noise outside the window. It sounded like rain, then it sounded like something else. I got up and peeped around the curtain out the window."

"Big, big snowflakes were falling hard and covering the ground white. I got excited. I went into the other bedroom and woke up Amelia Grai and Victoria Olivia."

"Come, see," he said. "Get up and look out the window."

"The girls got up and peeped out of the window. Victoria Olivia ran to the door and opened it. She ran outside. Amelia Grai and I ran outside too. We jumped over the bannister into the new snow," said Lil Mike.

"Are you kidding me?" I asked.

"Did you put your coat and shoes on?"

"Nope," said Amelia Grai. "We didn't think about our shoes or coat. We didn't know it was cold outside."

"The snow was up high and we just wanted to play in it. It was so pretty out there and the moon was shining. We could see it. It looked so soft. We ran out and jumped down in the snow," chimed Victoria Olivia.

"OH, you guys could have caught a cold," I said.

"We had our PJ's on and we were warm at first."

"Where were your parents," I asked.

"In the other bedroom asleep," said Lil Mike.

"You got those younger sisters in that mess, didn't you, Lil Mike."

"I did. It was fun," he said.

"I got cold that night. I wanted to go back in," said Victoria Olivia.

"We left the door wide open," said Amelia Grai.

"Good thing you did. You would have had to wake your parents up to get back inside."

"What time was it when you guys did this fool -hardy thing?" I asked.

"Around mid-night," answered Lil Mike. "We didn't do anything wrong. We just wanted to feel the snow. It was so pretty. WE had not seen snow like this before in New Orleans."

"Besides," said Amelia Grai, "we were so happy. We thanked God for the snow. We had seen snow men on TV around Christmas time but we did not know how to make one. We kept throwing the snow up in the air."

Victoria Olivia was the first child to admit that she was cold and wanted to go back inside.

"It wasn't cold to me. I wanted to stay out there," said Lil Mike.

"We went back inside our Condo and got back in bed," said Amelia Grai.

"We didn't catch cold or anything," said Lil Mike.

"Did you tell your parents the next day?" I asked.

"Nope, we never told them. That was our little fun time and our little secret."

"We never said one word about it," said Victoria Olivia tartly.

"Why are you telling me now?" I asked. It's several years later. We have gone to Gatlinburg three times because I have a Time Share there. I get two Condos each time so we can have enough rooms for the whole family."

"We're telling you now because you are our grandma and we know you won't spank us. Besides, we are older now, and we know better than to do it again," said Lil Mike.

Victoria Olivia said, "That was a long time ago. Grandma G. We're more grown-up now."

"Remember, kids often act like grown-ups and grown-up sometimes act like kids. Always act your age."

CHAPTER XIV

Next Day's Adventure

"WHAT DID YOU do next? What did you do the next day?" I asked.

I knew what they had done. I just wanted them to express themselves.

"We went to the Penguin Playhouse and played with the penguins. We took pictures with the penguins. We all went there. You were with us, Grandma G," said Victoria Olivia.

"Then, remember! We all went to 'Ripley's Believe It or Not.'

We saw so many unusual things in there. It's an internationally famous 'odditorium'. There were over 500 amazing exhibits in there. We stayed in there a half a day until we got really really hungry."

"How did you learn that word, 'ODDITORIUM,' Victoria Olivia?"

"I think I read it somewhere when we were out there," said Victoria Olivia.

"It was on a sign outside the 'Ripley's Believe It or Not' building," said Lil Mike.

"What did you do next?" I asked.

"Remember, Grandma G, we all met up and went to lunch at the Bennett's Pit Barbeque restaurant on River Road. Ooo, they had Hickory smoked barbeque beef, pork and chicken. Then they had a salad and soup-bar."

"Yah, Dad tore into that salad bar and got a big bowl of salad. He says he's always trying to lose weight," said Lil Mike.

Kiara said, "Cows eat grass all day and they stay fat. Lettuce is just like grass. The more you eat, the fatter you get."

The girls started laughing.

Victoria Olivia said, "I was watching Grandpa Bert. He went to the salad and soup -bar and got the biggest bowl of soup."

When he came back to the table, I said, "Oh, Grandpa, you like soup, don't you?"

He said, "I love soup. I eat a bowl of soup every night. Ask your Grandma!"

"After we ate at that restaurant, we went to Ripley's Aquarium of the Smokies," said Olivia Christina.

"Olivia, you were tiny. Mom was pushing you in a stroller. You remember that?" asked Lil Mike.

Olivia Christina said, "I remember everything. I saw the shark exhibit in the underwater tunnel, and the wide stingrays and the big old horseshoe crabs."

"They had a penguin show where they were feeding the penguins. There were lots of sea creatures and pretty fish. I remember all of it. Then I fell asleep. Daddy picked me up out of stroller and carried me on his shoulder."

Mike G, the little one's father, said "that was pretty neat, wasn't it? And Olivia Christina, you were the baby, yet you remembered all of that information."

"But going back to this playing in the snow," said Dad.

"I heard you telling Grandma G about it. I'm glad you prayed and thanked God for the snow. It is His creation."

"By the time we heard you come back into the Condominium and 'quietly' shut the door, I got up to see what was going on. All three of you were sound asleep. I decided to let sleeping dogs lie (take a nap)," said Mom.

Lil Mike said, "Dad and Mom, you knew all this time that we had played in the snow?"

"I didn't know how long you had been out there, I just knew that you had come back in and shut the door. I did not want to spoil the trip for the whole family, your grandparents, aunts and uncles and cousins by fussing at you. We were all having a good time," said Mike G.

Victoria Olivia said, "I really had a great time. We went to a 'Kickoff and Chili cookoff in our Condo play area and later a movie."

"I don't remember what movie we saw because I went to sleep after eating some popcorn. I was little, so Mom broke little pieces for me and put it in my mouth. I drank some Sprite from my sippy cup and went to sleep," said Olivia Christina.

"I had a lot of fun, too. The 'sky lift' was great. We could see the whole city from up in the sky."

"I was a little scared at first. Everyone else was sitting quietly in their chair and talking. So, I got OK!" said Amelia Grai.

"Dad, Uncle Keith and Uncle Albert went golfing one day. They came back to the Condos tired, but happy. They were laughing at how poorly they played golf," Lil Mike said.

"That's the day that Grandma G, Aunt Karen and Aunt Nancy took us to the Hypnotized Comedy show. We laughed and laughed at some of the things the man did to other people, then we let him try to blow our minds with some of his tricks," said Christian -Paris.

"Grandma G bought me a set of the trick box. The other kids did not want one. I tried a couple of tricks, then I put it away."

"One day while we were in Gatlinburg, we went to a Hollywood Star Car Museum. We saw super star cars from old movies and TV shows. They had music, sounds, lights and action from the movies to make it more authentic in the car museum."

"We could identify some of the shows that these cars were in," said Lil Mike.

"We saw the 'Fast and the Furious 5, Transformer, Dolly, Batmobile!"

"Man, I wanted to get in that Batmobile!" said Lil Mike. "They had a sign on it that said: 'Do not Touch!'

"I could understand why. That wasn't a car. That was a treasure," I said.

"I really enjoyed that part of the trip. I'm a car guru," laughed Lil Mike.

"They had cars from Ghostbusters, Beverly Hillbillies, Back to the Future, Batmobile -over 40 vehicles in that collection. I remember. I'm definitely a car guru!"

"Where did you get that term, Lil Mike?" I asked.

"Off of the TV," he said.

"What does it mean," asked Amelia Grai.

"It means "to be a leader or acknowledged advocate of a movement or an idea, a recognized leader or teacher.""

"I did my homework, Grandma G. I looked it up before I used the term. This is the first time I used it. It sounds almost right, doesn't it?" he said.

"I'm proud of you, Mikey (another nickname).

"You are doing fantastic," as Aunt Nancy always says.

"I remember we went to the NASCAR SPEEDPARK, said Christian-Paris. They put a wristband on your wrist and you could ride in the little car all day."

"Christian-Paris, your daddy Keith got into one. I fell out laughing before I got into mine. Grandpa Bert was the only one who did not get into a car. We rode around and around the SPEEDPARK."

"We rode around eight tracks. There was a fire breathing dragon and bumper boats. That was lots of fun."

"Grandma G, another thing that I enjoyed was the water rafting," said Nia Olivia.

"This was the first time I had ever gone rafting on the water rides. We went on the upper and lower Pigeon River on a large raft. All of us got on the raft to ride five miles down the river. It was so many of us in the family that two or three people said they would catch the next raft so we could all go together."

"After our water rafting ride, we went to the BUBBA GUMP restaurant."

"We had shrimp and broiled oysters and gumbo that I recognized from New Orleans. It felt like we were home because we are from New Orleans. The restaurant people were so friendly. They came and talked to us like the BUBBA GUMP restaurant people do in New Orleans," said Victoria Olivia.

"This is so fun," said Nia Olivia.

"I've never been in a BUBBA GUMP restaurant before," she said.

"We always try to find one where ever we go," said Victoria Olivia.

"Dad and Mom like the HARD ROCK Café, too, and we find one in all the towns we go to," said Olivia Christina.

We went to the Parrot Mountain and Garden of Eden in Pigeon Forge. Pigeon Forge is right near Gatlinburg. All kinds of beautiful birds, hundreds of tropical birds were in the Parrot Mountain. The children were walking up to some of the birds and touching them."

"I had never seen so many beautiful sights in the whole wide world," said Victoria Olivia.

"We touched some of them," said Victoria Olivia and Olivia Christina simultaneously. "Can you imagine that these birds have been around since the beginning of time," I said.

"In the beginning, God created all things." (Genesis 1: 1-31, NIV.)

"This is why I wanted my grandchildren to come to this place, to see the wonders of nature, the mountains and all of God's creation."

"There is another town near those other two towns called Sevierville. We haven't talked about it much. Sevierville is where our Condominium suites were," I said.

"We stepped out of our suites every night and went to the play rooms, movies and pool tables."

"It was so much to see. We knew we were going to come back to Gatlinburg, Pigeon Forge and Sevierville for more fun."

CHAPTER XV

Christian-Paris' Eagle Scout Celebration

ONE NEVER FORGETS the first time something happens to him. Moreover, there are occasions in one's life that will only happen once. This is true with becoming an Eagle Scout.

Under the leadership of Pastor Roosevelt Wright, Jr., Christian-Paris became an Eagle Scout three days before his eighteenth birthday on December 9, 2018. He began his journey as a Boy Scout (Cub Scout) in the Top Gun Leadership Academy program nine years ago.

Keith Phenix, II, Christian-Paris' step brother, was a member of the Top Gun Leadership Academy, as well.

Five years ago, our family began hearing rumblings about Christian-Paris becoming an Eagle Scout. His mother and father, Karen and Keith were excited about the whole process and did everything to assist their child with this endeavor.

Christian-Paris is standing on the shoulders of giants: his two uncles, Bertrand II and Michael Gerard Griffin were Boy Scouts, his two great uncles, George and Daniel Heath were Boy Scouts. Even his grandfather, Bertrand Griffin, Sr. was a Boy Scout. His cousin, Michael Gerard Griffin, II had the opportunity of being a Boy Scout.

Christian-Paris is the only member of the Griffin/Heath/Phenix family to become an Eagle Scout.

This is the first Eagle Scout ceremony our family has ever attended. It was magnificent and heartwarming. Of course, we are only grandparents, but we were so excited that night.

Michael Hayatt, in his book, YOUR BEST YEAR EVER, pronounces, "Life throws curveballs."

Hayatt continues, "Whatever has happened in your past – good or bad- it's truly possible to make this your best year ever. Even in those areas where you've suffered setbacks and serious self-doubts, the current year can be the most meaningful and significant year in your life thus far." (p.18.)

"Christian-Paris, remember we have taught you the biblical scripture, "I can do all things through Christ who strengthens me," said Karen, his mother.

In other words, "we know that in all things, God works for the good of those who love Him, who are called according to His purpose. For those, God knew he had also predestined them to be confirmed to the likeness of his son, that he might be the first born among many brothers. And those He predestined, he also called; those he called, he justified; those he justified, He also glorified." (Romans 8: 28-30, NIV.)

"What then, shall we say in response to this? If God is for us, who can be against us."

There are times in all of God's children when we are called on to suffer. We read in Romans 5:3-4 "that suffering produces perseverance, perseverance, character, and character, hope."

"While believers are sustained in their suffering by hope, we are also sustained in our weakness in the most special way of all:

"The Spirit helps us in our weakness.
We do not know what we ought to pray for,
But the Spirit Himself intercedes for us
with groans that words cannot express.
And He who searches our hearts,
Knows the mind of the Spirit,
Because the Spirit intercedes for
the saints in accordance with God's will."
(Romans 8: 26-27, NIV.)

"Imagine, Christian-Paris, you have an abiding sense of opportunity in your life to become whatever you desire to be."

"For the moment, I want you to consider what a truly breakthrough year might look like for you. Your life is full of promise and purpose for even brighter days and a bigger story."

When Christian-Paris was studying to go before the Boy Scout Committee Review Board for the level of Eagle Scout, he called upon his uncle, Bertrand, II for help. Bertrand II, a pilot and member of the Black Pilots of America, New Orleans Golden Eagle chapter, (and his wife Kotasha an associate member) was a Boy Scout leader several years in Kennewick, Washington. He had much knowledge and skills and was a tremendous help to Christian-Paris.

As I discussed the Boy Scouts of America with Bertrand II and Christian-Paris, I learned much more than I knew as a Den Mother. I served in this capacity when Bertrand, II was about eight years old with Allen Martin, who was the Scout leader at our St. Mark United Methodist church.

Boy Scouting is a very dynamic program. When a young boy joins a unit, he does not have rank. As he gains knowledge and participates in projects, he becomes a person who earns badges through his service in Cub Scouting. The ranks are as follows:

1. Bob Cat
2. Tiger Cub
3. Wolf
4. Bear
5. We Be Lo S (Will Be Loyal Scout.)
6. Arrow of Light

As he/she continues into Boy Scout, the Arrow of Light prepares the young person for Boy Scout ranks:

1. Tenderfoot
2. Second Class
3. First Class
4. Star
5. Life

6. Eagle Scout*

> After the three ranks and the earning of badges,
> Christian-Paris was given additional leadership roles. Then
> he became a Patrol Leader during his last three ranks,
> earning badges as he went.
> He had to earn at least thirty-five badges before he went
> before the Board of Review to become an Eagle Scout.

> Christian-Paris had many experiences in his young life
> both as a Boy Scout as well as his other endeavors. As a
> child, Christian-Paris played soccer, basketball, baseball and
> football. He also trained in karate and swimming.

"His parents talked time and time again about the wisdom, skills and knowledge he gained. He also gained practical knowledge, maturity and good judgement and had a few struggles as he moved into his dream of becoming an Eagle Scout."

Sometimes as he talked to us, his grandparents, it appeared that he wanted to give up. Sometime, the road was rocky and uneven. He felt that everything was too hard.

A great philosopher, St. Athanaseus, once said, "When we dream, the soul transcends the body, and holds divine communication with the angels."

One skill that Christian-Paris learned was to write his thoughts and stories in journals and in a book along with his fellow members of Boy Scout Troop 65 and its 'Venture Crew.'

His chapter in the book, TIME TRAVELER TALES, was entitled 'Twelve in Space,' revealing that at an early age, he had a great desire and dream to travel into outer space."

"A story about space travel, Christian-Paris Griffin, 12 years old, included a fantasy odyssey about a twelve-year-old stowaway on a space shuttle."

"This collection of short stories focused on the state of Florida. The book was published by Pastor Roosevelt Wright, Scout Leader of the Top Gun Leadership Program."

Christian-Paris' fascinating story began, "The black void in space went on forever. I sat in the rocket ship and looked out of the portal. I was weightless and had to hold on to keep myself from bumping around. I was impressed with the vastness and blackness of space," he said.

"Each year, Top Gun Academy youth travel throughout the United States studying the history and cultural mix of America, reading, studying and learning about their destinations. Their excursions include ten to fourteen states each year, including Hawaii and Alaska, with the attempt to cover all fifty states, learning and reading about them and other issues that concern the United States of America."

This group has been featured in the International SCOUTING MAGAZINE** as 'Time Travelers' because of their extensive tours and studies of the United States."

Christian-Paris learned that "God can use anyone to touch someone else, if you are willing to listen and heed his call."

Miranda Kerr once more indicated in her book, TREASURE YOURSELF, "Take time to work out what really excites and inspires you. Discover what you would be prepared to do every day even for free. When you are following your passion, it won't even seem like work to you."

She goes on to say," "Passionate people feel alive with their unwavering sense of direction in life." (p. 75.)

Keith, Christian-Paris' father said, "Think of yourself as having the tools you need in life and set your goals to achieve what you want in life."

Christian earned his Eagle Scout badge by leading a project at the Ronald McDonald House in Monroe, Louisiana. He worked with professional landscapers in completing a plan and design of landscaping the exterior of Ronald McDonald House.

He raised his money through donations and support from two churches, New Tabernacle Baptist Church in Monroe, which is pastored by Rev. Roosevelt Wright, Jr. The other church, St Mark United Methodist Church in Baton Rouge, Louisiana, is pastored by Rev. Dr. Derrick Hills.

Christian-Paris received commendations from the Ronald McDonald House. The staff also attended his Eagle Scout ceremony and thanked him for a project well done.

SOURCE: **www.scouting.org

CHAPTER XVI

Grandpa Bert Speaks

GRANDPA BERT ENTERED the conversation. "Children, you are blessed with good parents and grandparents. You must develop helpful habits in order to succeed in life."

"You -all, Grandpa Bert didn't eat very much. He has been waiting to speak," said Christian -Paris. I have been watching him."

"You're right, Bubby." (That's Grandpa Bert's nick-name for Christian-Paris since he was a baby.) "I'm full. I feel wonderful. There are so many beautiful sights around me. God has blessed me. I stayed awake last night until mid-night. When I saw my eighty-fourth birthday, I started singing this song.

> "When I see Jesus, AMEN.
> When I see Jesus, AMEN
> He bore my burdens in the heat of the day,
> I knew the Lord would make a way.
> When I see Jesus, AMEN."

"I kept singing it over and over until I fell asleep," Grandpa Bert mused.

"First you woke me up by singing it," I said. "After I sang it with you, then you went to sleep."

"Right," said Grandpa Bert.

"I truly have that attitude of gratitude today. Let me tell you just how significant this day is to me."

"My father, Roby Griffin, lived to be ninety -four years old. My mother, Annie Gillespie Griffin lived to be seventy -three. My grandmother, Minerva Griffin, lived to be seventy-six and her mother,

Mama Fannie Tessier Jones lived to be seventy-two. She was born in eighteen fifty-three and died in nineteen thirty-two."

"I'm eighty-four years old today. I have miles and miles to go before I sleep. I am overwhelmed by all the miracles I have experienced and seen in my lifetime.

First, my marriage to Grandma Marian was a miracle. I have always told people that our marriage was made in heaven."

I said, "He said it so much that I began to believe it."

"Then my children were miracles. Now, how about my beautiful grandchildren- all miracles!"

Grandpa Bert got up from the table and went to his rocking chair.

"I have found out that the greatest challenges in life can lead to the greatest successes," he said.

"I want to tell you a story that Rick McKinley, in his book, THIS BEAUTIFUL MESS, paraphrased from the Bible."

> "One day a messenger from God stood on a hillside. He was surrounded by a crowd of sweaty, hungry, desperate people: men women, old people, lovers, and kids.
>
> "As he looked into their eyes, He saw a question: 'Are you the one'?"
>
> "And behind the question, He saw longing! Longing for the ONE to come and explain why the world was in such a wreck. Longing for rescue, for healing, for one moment of insight that would change it all."
>
> "Longing for their one true King to show up and reclaim His kingdom, to kick the Roman occupiers out and make everything right again."
>
> "Jesus looked into their eyes and told them stories."
>
> "The Kingdom of Heaven is like yeast that a woman took and mixed into a large amount of flour until it worked all though the dough."
>
> "The Kingdom of Heaven is like a mustard seed which a man took and planted in his field. Though it was the smallest of all seeds, yet when it grows, it is the largest of

garden plants and becomes a tree, so that the birds of the air come and perch in its branches."

"Granddaddy, you rock!" said Christian-Paris.

Grandpa Bert said, I'm just quoting the Bible and the writer. One more story!"

"The Kingdom of Heaven is like a treasure hidden in a field. When a man found it, he hid it again. Then in his joy, he went and sold all he had, and bought that field." (p. 12.)

Grandpa Bert, I don't understand some of His stories. I know it is Jesus telling them, but I don't get it," said Lil Mike.

"The people did not get it either. They don't get it now."

"The people in Jesus' day listened to every word out in the hot sun."

"The Kingdom, He said, is powerful, invasive and unbelievably beautiful. The Kingdom is waiting to be discovered in the dirt of their everyday lives."

"It is the prize worth waiting for."

With each story the people were thinking, "Yes, Yes. That's it! That's exactly what we want."

"And could He be the ONE?"

"Their longing deepened."

For the next three years, Jesus spread the good news, telling stories and parables to the people.

"Speaking in homes, on roadsides, from boats, in synagogues, He spread the good news of the Kingdom. Kingdom they understood. After all, they lived in a world defined by kings and emperors. Some of His hearers heard, and believed. Others turned away." (McKinley, p 13.)

"Our stories of failure can be God's stories of success. Look for God's purpose in your next interruption."

"I no longer live, but Christ lives in me. The life I live in the body, I live by faith in the Son of God, who loved me and gave Himself for me." (Galatians 2: 20.)

MARIAN OLIVIA HEATH GRIFFFIN

"My children and grandchildren, you are my greatest assets. Therefore, the more we invest in you, the greater the benefits and rewards we receive when we witness your successes."

Grandpa Bert said, "Marian, your mother/grandmother said, "A good education is the key to much of our success, and my sixth generation ancestor, Mama Fannie Tessier, who was a slave in the mid- 1800's realized that her children and grandchildren had to get an education in order to succeed in life."

"We as black people cannot get jobs today. Our children and grandchildren cannot get good jobs because we are not training our children or helping them get a high school education and college degree."

"I read an article the other day that we need to get serious about getting an education in order to close the job-market gap," I said.

"I have always been concerned about our children getting educated, just as our parents were concerned about us getting a good education," said Grandpa Bert.

"Your Grandma G started an IRA-Educational savings account for each of you grandchildren. She wanted you to have every benefit of going to college and having a better life than you would have if you did not get an education."

Grandpa Bert said, "My mother insisted that my two siblings and I go to college. She believed in private schools. She sent my sister, Darcus and brother Amos to Leland College in Baker and sent me to Dillard University in New Orleans," Grandpa Bert said.

My mother had attended Straight College in New Orleans which later became Dillard University. When your parents, Bertrand II and Michael Gerard finished high school, they both wanted to attend Dillard University," said Grandpa Bert.

"I know why," I said. "Every time we went to New Orleans, Grandpa Bert started singing "Fair Dillard, Gleaming White and Spacious Green. This was Dillard's Alma Meter song."

"I loved my school," said Grandpa Bert. Everyone was laughing.

"Our sons' brains got connected to Dillard University when they were young. Karen wanted to go to a school in New Orleans, but she chose Xavier University. All's well that ends well."

CHAPTER XVII

Kiara's Expressions – High School Graduation

"ALL I CAN tell you is that my high school graduation was the best day of my life. I had started jotting down goals for my life- things that I wanted to do, a wish list," said Kiara.

"When I walked across that stage and accepted that diploma from my mom, I wanted to shout and yell, 'Hallelujah, Praise the Lord.'

"Just to let you know, my mom was a principal of a school but not my high school."

"Her best friend, who was the principal of my high school, had a daughter who was a student at my mom's school. The other daughter was graduating too from my mom's school."

"The two principals, my mom and her best friend, got permission from the school board office to switch school graduations, so that they could give their own daughter her diploma," said Kiara.

Splendid idea! "That's a fantastic story and both mothers and daughters had memorable and unforgettable occasions.

Richard Blanco said in his book, FOR ALL OF US, ONE TODAY, "Every story begins inside a story that's already begun by others." (5.)

"Long before we took our first breath, there was a situation well underway with character and a setting we did not choose, but which was chosen for us." (p. 6.)

"God has plans and he provides comfort in His messages. He brings friends together and has a way of performing miracles in our lives that we have no clue will remind us of who He is."

"He is our creator, our maker and way maker. He makes a way out of no way and helps us to solve our problems if we just let Him."

"Yes," said Grandpa Bert. "I was there at your graduation, Kiara. It is unbelievable how big the world is and how great our minds are. The story was told to us that night about how the two principals switched schools to preside over their respective daughters' graduations."

"Yes, the world is big, our minds are great. But God is bigger. It is a wonderful thing to be made whole and full. This means we can stop searching for self-worth in the elemental and base philosophies of the world. Our future is complete and sure in Christ because no longer are we helpless in the face of an unseen destiny."

"He is before all things, and in Him all things hold together. He is the Head of the body...."

(Colossians 1: 17-18, NIV.)

"Kiara," I said. "You wanted to yell and holla across that stage when you got your diploma."

"We did yell. We were hollering, 'Go, Kiara. Go, Shawana.' Nia Olivia was sitting near us. She and her friends were screaming your name. We were so happy for you. 'Stonewall' Bertrand II even let out a hoot."

"You may not have heard us, but we meant our sentiment as an act of encouragement."

Paul said, "Encourage one another and build each other up." (1 Thessalonians 5: 11, NIV.)

"Now we are looking forward to your college days."

"Kiara, you have a new work to do now. You said that you had made a wish list years ago. Now it is time to make it real and reach for your dreams."

Charles E. Blake stated in his book FREE TO DREAM, that biblical persons succeeded based on their actual dreams. You must make your dream list, now."

"Blake stated "Before we talk about reaching for our dreams, we need to define what dreams are not. First, dreams are not wishes.

"I wish I had a million dollars," I've heard many people say.

"Lining up to buy lotto tickets when the prize reaches unusually large numbers creates a lotto fever. Normal, average people take their grocery money and their mortgage payment to buy lotto tickets with the hopes and wishes of becoming millionaires."

"A wish is a passing fancy, an idle thought, or a whim without consequences or impact. A wish carries no weight and packs no punch. It's spoken and gone in a second." (Blake, p. 18.)

"Dreams are real. They are not whimsical wishes. A dream without a godly goal and a righteous plan of action is a fantasy."

"You may realize that we all have roles to play and we are all unique. We have different gifts, talents, visions and abilities," I said.

"All generations are searching for answers and looking for them in the lives of high-profile individuals whom society lifts as role models," said James Brown in his book, ROLE OF A LIFE TIME.

Johnathan Swift states in his narrative, THOUGHTS ON VARIOUS SUBJECTS, "Visions are the art of seeing things invisible."

"God often uses our gifts, our abilities, our talents and our prayers in unexpected ways to help us learn and grow into who He wants us to be. It is the answer or change He helps us accept because He wants to transform us with His love."

Mariana M. Cooper, in her book, THE AHA FACTOR, stated, "We all have something major to contribute in life and many of us never do." (p. 8.)

"Grandma G, you surely read a lot of books, don't you!"

"Kiara, what I enjoy about reading now is that I can read what I want to read, not assigned readings. When I was in school and had assigned readings, I was learning to read what I wanted to read.

I chose my careers early in life, first music and social work, then music and psychological counseling, then music and writing books and news articles. What I am trying to tell you is, you may have had many wants and wishes. Time now to turn those wishes into the dreams and passion to do with your life what you want to do."

Cooper went on to say, "That is why letting your dreams and deepest longings come to the fore-front that is a much bigger picture that you fit into and your dreams are not only important for you, but also for the world at large."

"Dreaming enables us to pray to God for the big things and the little things. Two famous dreamers in the Bible were Joseph and Daniel. My mother named her two younger sons after these two dreamers."

"Another well-known dreamer was noted in the Bible for saying:

"Your sons and daughters will prophesy,
Your old men will dream dreams,
Your young men (and women) will see visions,
Even on my servants, both men and women,
I will pour out my Spirit in those days.
I will show wonders in the heaven and on the earth,
.....And everyone who calls on the name of the Lord
will be saved."
(Joel 2: 28-32, NIV.)

"I appreciate the 'Black Lives Matter' and 'All Lives Matter'. Seemingly, it takes someone else to tell us that our lives matter and what we do with our lives matters. All our lives do matter and should matter to us most of all."

"God made us all. And, I'm just going to go there!"

"GOD DID NOT MAKE BUT ONE BLOOD! We divided it up into little parts and pieces," I said.

"That's a whole new book!"

"Wait for it!"

"Moving right along, It's your life for the rest of your life. Don't just have sleeping dreams. Have prayerful dreams. Have working dreams. You have completed high school. That's a fantastic first start. Trust and believe in God to work with and through you to accomplish your goals," I said.

"You inspire the rest of the family with your tenacity and grit, your ability to meet challenges and struggles and work through them with God's help," I said.

"In college, you will be staying up all night, burning the mid-night oil to do what you need to do and get where you want to be. Gaining valuable insight and accepting yourself, upping your own self-esteem are the keys you will need. You may be rough around the edges at first, but dare to give yourself skills and abilities to succeed."

"I can agree with Kerr. You are an amazing, unique and talented young woman in this world. Through your own journey of self-discovery, you may come to see just how incredible you really are."

"Take yourself serious but not too seriously. Work hard in college and have lots of fun. I did!"

CHAPTER XVIII

The Halloween Mini Bus

VICTORIA OLIVIA AND Amelia Grai were sitting near Grandpa Bert. They started asking him questions.

Amelia Grai said, "Grandpa Bert, you and Grandma G visit us every Christmas and bring us gifts and presents and food."

"We get excited when we know you and Grandma G are coming. Besides Christmas, what other holiday do you like to come and visit us?"

"That's a loaded question, Amelia Grai. You're about to run me up a tree."

"I enjoy every holiday and all my other visits with you. I remember one occasion that was unique to me. When each of you were smaller, we came to every birthday party. We had Easter egg hunts in our back yard and in our house. Your Grandmother and I tried to hide an equal number of eggs for each of you and help the youngest children find their eggs."

"I remember one of the most enjoyable parties that we attended that was unique to me. That was the Halloween party on the Mini bus in New Orleans."

"Grandpa Bert, you remember that Halloween party?" Lil Mike came over to join the conversation.

"Man! That was something! We had a lot of fun. I was in charge!" said Lil Mike.

"I let Christian-Paris help, since he was the other big boy in the bunch."

"You can help me tell the story, Mike, since you were in change," said Grandpa Bert.

"Ok, it was Halloween night, six o'clock in the evening. My four sisters and eleven cousins climbed on a chartered Mini bus at our house in New Orleans."

I said, "I remember that Mini bus ride. Grandpa Bert and Papa J.V. and I climbed on first and went all the way to the back of the bus."

"I was heisting the little children up and Aunt Tracie and Uncle Mike were getting them seated," said Christian-Paris.

"Mikey was telling them where to sit. He was in charge," said Christian -Paris.

"He and Aunt Tracie had planned the whole trip, whose houses to go to and where to stop to get their trick or treat goodies."

"We picked up our big cousins, Nia Olivia and Kiara Janelle who jumped on the front seats. There was much excitement and giggling."

Mikey took the microphone; he was the master of ceremony. He announced where the children were to get on and off the bus. It was dark so all we could see were buildings. There were specific houses and the Mini bus driver knew where to stop.

Big Mike, the father of the smaller children was the Captain of the ship, 'oups', I mean the Mini bus.

Tracie was the General- in- charge. Each person had their assignments. Each child had a seat assignment. Most of us boarded the bus outside of Big Mike's house. Then we picked up a few more children.

As we rode along the streets of New Orleans, Mikey announced landmarks. Some places were lit up like it was Christmas. These were the relatives' home that we stopped at and the children went in to get their 'trick or treat.' Twelve pre-planned family and friend homes were the 'trick or treat' stops.

The grandparents sat on the back seats and observed. Papa J.V. was from New Orleans, so he had the advantage of knowing all the houses and the streets.

Grandpa Bert had attended Dillard University in New Orleans and I had attended New Orleans Baptist Theological Seminary and had worked as a social worker in New Orleans.

So, the old folk knew some of the landmarks that we saw.

The children climbed on and off the Mini bus. It was warm inside the bus and chilly outside. After all, it was the last day of October. The children took their coats and hats off in the bus and we had to scramble to help them put the coats and hats back on to get off the bus.

It was work, but it was fun. The children were so excited. Everyone was in a good mood. The children were ecstatic about hollowing 'Trick or Treat' and the candy and toys and money they were receiving.

The children's treats were given to Mom Tracie and Dad Mike G to be redistributed at the end of the Halloween Mini bus ride.

The last stop was made at the Dookie Chase restaurant. Great Grandmother Leah Chase, her husband, Dookie II and the restaurant staff had been awaiting the little 'Trick or Treaters' all night.

When we arrived, Grandmother Chase was standing at the door giving each one of her grands and great grandchildren hugs and kisses. She sent them inside to get their treats and their goodie bags. Each child came out of the restaurant licking an ice cream cone and carrying a small bag of cookies along with a big goodie bag which was collected at the Mini bus door by the ship Captain and the General-in Charge.

After the final stop at the Dookie Chase Restaurant, the children clambered back on the Mini bus and started singing nursery songs. Some of them fell asleep on the ride home. The cousin's parents and grandparents were waiting at Michael and Tracie's house.

TGIF! Thank God it was Friday night and the children did not have school the next day. And a good time was had by all!

CHAPTER XIX

Ripley's Haunted House Adventure

WHEN WE WERE in Gatlinburg in 2010, we had some experiences that we should never forget.

This was our second trip to Gatlinburg, the Great Smoky Mountain National Park.

"I had an apparition or dream the other night about one of the experiences Christian -Paris and I had in Gatlinburg. The Gatlinburg Vacation Guide called it RIPLEY'S HAUNTED ADVENTURE," I said.

"It seemed to be a maze with red dots, because that is what I saw in that house."

About ten years ago the family took their annual vacation in Gatlinburg, Tenn. The group included Mike's seven family members, Bertrand's four family members, Karen's three family members, Aunt Nancy and uncle Albert and Grandpa Bert and me.

Mike, Tracie and their five children require their own Condo. The rest of the family share a three- or four-bedroom Condo which is sufficient.

The second day of our five-day vacation was spent exploring the area. We all went into the RIPLEY'S BELIEVE IT OR NOT and spent about three hours in there. We had lunch in one of the restaurants called 'The Mountain Edge Grill.'

We enjoyed whatever our taste buds called for: buffalo burgers, large and small pizza's which were shared, a variety of sandwiches, appetizers, soups and salads. We experienced a great mountain lodge atmosphere and left happy and full.

After lunch, the family members split up to explore different attractions.

Christian-Paris wanted to go into the Haunted House called "An Adventure in Fear." Karen and Keith, Christian-Paris' parents did not want to go into the Haunted House.

I agreed to go in with him. A sign said, 'Children under six years old were not admitted."

Christian-Paris was eight years old, so he had just made it. His birthday was in a few days.

I asked, "Christian, do you remember that experience?"

"Was it scary, Christian? We were too young to go in," said Lil Mike.

Christian-Paris said, "my parents did not want to go in either."

Granny said, "I'll go in with you."

"She took me in there. We paid our fare at the window and the man opened the gate to let us in," Christian said.

As soon as we got in, it was dark, dark in there. We saw other people going in ahead of us.

"We heard people laughing and talking. Then we did not hear any more people. We heard other animal sounds."

"I really remember, now" said Christian-Paris. "We were scared inside. It was supposed to be unique and scary fun. It was advertised as having live actors and special effects."

"It was pitch dark in there. The only lights that we saw were little red lights on the floor," I said.

"My mother had always taught me, 'look to the light."

"When something frightens you, 'look to the light."

"It may be the moon shining through a window, 'look to the light."

"In the haunted House, we were walking in total darkness, bumping into what seemed like fences and walls. Once in a while, we saw a mirror where we could see our reflection in the dark."

"We heard people talking at first, then we heard only animal sounds like a cow mooing, or a horse whinnying or a lion roaring. We even heard an elephant make a high pitch sound. The ground was uneven."

"We seemed to be touching things. There were walls."

"I started saying, "Keep going, Christian-Paris. Keep going and look to the light."

"I don't see any light, Granny and I'm scared."

"Hold my hand."

"Granny, there are no lights, only red dots on the floor."

"Let's try to get out of here. Your parents will think we are lost or disappeared into thin air."

I couldn't see my watch. It felt like we had been in the haunted house for hours.

Christian-Paris said, "I'm really scared, Granny."

That's the first time I realized that Christian was calling me Granny. He has called me that ever since. He used to call me Grandma G.

"I don't know why the name 'Granny' gave me courage, but it did."

I started praying. "Deliver us, Lord," I said silently over and over.

"Christian, I saw a little light in one of the corners. I thought it was a mirror, because I thought I could see myself. I looked weird."

"I saw that too, but I didn't say anything. I didn't want to frighten you."

"Creedie Pete' (my nick-name for Christian-Paris), I'm supposed to be in here protecting you. And you're trying to protect me."

"Granny, we're in this boat together. Let's paddle our way out of here," said Christian-Paris.

"We were trying to encourage each other throughout this whole ordeal. I was thinking, there will be moments where we falter and need someone to help us or pick us up. At other times, someone may need our encouragement through our presence and prayers."

Ecclesiastes said it best: "Two are better than one….if either of them falls down, one can help the other up." (Eccl. 4: 9-12, NIV.)

"God does not want us to run this race alone. He is leading you into someone else's life. Let us finish our task together."

After 'hours' in the Haunted House of Fear, Creedie Pete and I back-tracked in the darkness and found the little crack in the wall again.

I couldn't see my hand, let alone my watch. I didn't know what time it was. We had gone into the haunted house around one o'clock.

We both pushed on the wall where there was a crack.

We almost fell over, stepping out of the crack in the wall or 'maze' as I called it.

When we got outside, there was more difficulty. The sun was so bright, my eyes were dilatating. Christian-Paris closed his eyes. Karen, his mother ran and caught him.

"Christian-Paris, can you see?" she asked.

"What happened?"

Christian-Paris replied, "No, I can't see, so I just closed my eyes."

Karen and Keith were sitting on a wooden bench a little ways down from where we came out of the Haunted House. The building looked so different from the one we went into.

Christian was only eight years old. He was kind of sniffling. Karen grabbed his hand.

"What happened in there? You Guys looked so scared when you came out. We thought you were going to come out on the other end. You came out the same door that you went into."

"We were scared," said Christian-Paris.

"I thought we would never get out. It felt like we were in a world of darkness all by ourselves for hours and hours," I said.

"You were in there for only about ten minutes," Keith said.

"It felt like a whole day. We were in total darkness. There were no other people in there but us, even though we saw people go in ahead of us," said Christian-Paris.

"We heard them talking and laughing for a few minutes, then we couldn't hear them anymore."

"We heard only animal noises and I felt something touching me."

"We heard a lot of loud laughter and other funny sounds."

"Christian-Paris and I were walking, sometimes almost crawling on our knees. Where were all of the other people who had gone into the haunted house ahead of us. There were persons standing behind us waiting to get in. Where were they?"

"I was thinking all kinds of thoughts, wondering what kind of circumstances we had gotten ourselves into. Should we go forward or back-track? I had a small child with me. This situation was just for fun. Why am I so stressed out?"

I put on my philosophical cap.

"What would Margaret Mead, one of my heroines, blind at birth and a missionary, say or do."

She would say, "Never doubt that a small group of people can change the world. Indeed, it is the only thing that ever has."

"Karen," I told my daughter, "that was the most frightful thing I have ever done, even though I have been in other haunted houses and fun houses and much worse spots than that, especially physical danger, but this was playing with my mind. My mother always said, "don't let no one mess with your mind, "I said.

When the writer of Ecclesiastes, Solomon, grappled over the problems and frustrations of the world, he realized that one person may "be overpowered, but two can defend themselves." (Ecc. 4: 9, NIV.)

"A friend nearby can help us up when we fall down and encourage us to travel the journey together with others, so we don't have to face the trials of life alone. Having a teammate or a friend to share or be around us is the best strategy for facing struggles or trials that we bear. Moreover, we must never give up the attempt or endeavor to reach our goal."

"I heard somewhere in my life from one of my many military family members that in the Army everyone has a 'battle buddy.' I guess that Christian-Paris was my 'battle -buddy,' and I was his that day.

"A cord of three strands is not quickly broken." (Ecc. 4: 12, NIV.)

"God is never going to make a mistake with his motif that He has especially designed for us."

"The Lord guarantees that all crisis already has been met and overcome in Him."

Keith suggested, "Let's go get some hamburgers and fries. That'll calm us all down."

Christian-Paris started laughing. "Yah, let's go, Dad, because I'm starving."

FAST FORWARD:

"That was a real haunted house," said Kiara. "I'm glad we did not go in there. Dad asked us if we wanted to go in, but Nia and I said, "no."

Nia Olivia said," I've been in a haunted house before. But it wasn't that scary. The one I went into was fun to me."

I said, "If purgatory is anything like that, I definitely do not want to go there."

Amelia Grai and Victoria Olivia said simultaneous, "What is purgatory, Grandma G?"

"Ok, dictionary time."

Lil Mike said, "I'll find the dictionary. You find the word, Amelia."

"Amelia Grai began reading, 'purgatory means, 'a place of suffering, expiation or remorse. A state in which the souls of those who have died in grace must expiate their sins before attaining heaven.'"

"Grandma G, if going to purgatory is the only way to get to heaven, you might want to reconsider."

"WoW!" You kids are deep. Let me reconsider that, please. I definitely want to go to heaven."

"Maybe that was why I was praying so hard in that haunted house."

Christian-Paris said, "I was praying hard, too."

"I think God made us turn around and seek a way out or we would have been in there until night time when they closed down."

"Grandma G, what made you think of the haunted house ten years later and remind us of it?"

"I never heard you tell that story before, Grandma G. I don't think I was born than. So, you would have had to tell me about it and I haven't heard that one," said Olivia Christina.

"Where did it happen? she asked.

"It happened in Gatlinburg: I think on our first trip."

Christian-Paris said, "Only Granny remembered it like she told it, even though I was with her."

"Cretie Pete, I had not thought about that experience for years. I just began dreaming about it two nights ago before you came over to see Grandpa Bert for his birthday."

God and the hamburger saved the day," said Christian-Paris.

"When we got back to our Condo that day, I started making a large pot of Gumbo. The adults in the room cut up the seasoning and chattered. It was a good day after all."

"Yes, God understands everything. Jesus was sent here on earth to experience life as a human being. Jesus is the one who can say, "I have experienced difficulties of the burning sun, a hungry stomach, the fright of the unknown, a feeling of loneliness and homelessness as well as love and friendship of family."

"I came to give you hope over your challenges and struggles. When you feel discouraged and tired, I came to help you have faith and listen to the calling of God."

MARIAN OLIVIA HEATH GRIFFFIN

CHAPTER XX

Nia Olivia's First College Day

NIA OLIVIA SAID, "I am going to talk about my first day in college since I am the only college kid in the room."

"I know that my 'Griffin scholarship' as Grandma G called it, really helped me and my parents get me through school. I will be a senior next year in an all-girl's school in Gainesville, Georgia. My school was by no means cheap and I know my parents and grandparents and other relatives sacrificed for me even though I had two athletic scholarships and one academic scholarship. It was not just tuition. There are so many other variables and issues when a person goes to college. There were new clothes, a car and travel money, books and supplies, many personal items, all kind of stuff.

"I thank you, Grandma G for saving money in an account for my college education. It has helped my parents and me abundantly."

Your godmother and other relatives sent money to me to put into your account once in a while. It helped. That is why I ask you to sometimes just call your relatives. They just wanted to let you know that they believed in you and your abilities. They sent money for a book or two.

"Nia Olivia, we need to have this conversation again and again with your sister and little cousins so they can digest it. You are their close-up mentor. They can see what you are doing. You are their up-close millennial or young adult. Everyone is looking to the next generation, the millennials for safety and a better future."

"What was your first day like in college, Nia," asked Victoria Olivia.

"I remember my first day in college. It seemed like my whole family came to see me off to college."

"My Griffin grandparents were there, my mother, my father and my sister were there. I agree, I was overwhelmed," said Nia Olivia.

"My mother's parents- Eugene and Bettye Redmond had passed away. We were very close to my other grandmother, Bettye, because she stayed with us several years before she died."

"I was not going to see my family everyday as I normally did when I was in elementary and high school. I thought that was going to be my biggest adjustment. I had one friend who was also on a track team from high school days. She was my roommate. Other than this friend, I did not know anyone."

Grandpa Bert said, "I hasten to say, we are so proud of you and want all of our grandchildren to follow in your footsteps, Nia Olivia."

"Always stand up for what you believe in. You are our first grandchild."

"Let us not be weary in doing good for at the proper time, we will reap a harvest if we do not give up. Therefore, as we have opportunity, let us do good." (Galatians 6; 9-10, NIV.)

"Nia Olivia, I know you had some trying times in school, but you are almost finished with that phase of your education," Grandpa Bert said.

"You are headed in the right direction," I said.

"Trust in the Lord with all your heart and lean not on your understanding. In all your ways acknowledge Him, and He will direct your path." (Proverb 3: 5-6, NIV.)

"Grandma G, when I grow up, I want to be just like Nia Olivia. She is my favorite cousin and she is showing us how to get a good education and how to act," said Olivia Christina.

Nia Olivia said, "The other day I heard a man say on TV that he was privileged 'to be white' like no other race was available. And he had great wealth and good health."

I said, "Did he mention that he had loving parents and grandparents? Did he indicate that God was in his life.?"

"Did he mention that he had brilliant ancestors like Mama Fannie Tessier and Lettie Heath and Rev. Allen Sam Gillespie? Did he subdue suppression and endure hardships and cruel hate and trauma due to his race?" I asked.

"He was privileged of his own volition, it appeared."

"I said, "We can trace our footsteps and our heritage because our privileges came as a result of being obedient especially to God."

"I understand what he meant but he did not take into consideration his own self-worth, his psychological wellbeing and social response to our society. He did not take into account the fact that God is the creator of us all."

"What did he have to fear? What would he have to give up to be a whole privileged person in the sight of God?"

"OH, there is much to be considered in claiming that you are privileged."

"How did we get off on that subject? It's deep," Uncle Keith said.

Aunt Karen asked, "Anyone want ice cream or cake?"

Karen has a knack for changing the subject.

The subject was considered changed. Everyone was ready for dessert. The adults were scrambling to get more food.

"Nia Olivia, my little god-child, I know you have not finished your story about your first college day."

"Carry on!" said Aunt Karen.

Nia Olivia said, "A lot was going on that first day, meeting with the financial people, my track team and coach, just a lot to do that week-end. Then I had to consider my parent's feelings; that there was separation anxiety in both of them as well. I knew my grandparents were going to be OK because they had put their own three children in college a long time ago."

"There were many dynamics and variables to think about. However, I was glad to be going to college."

"Nia Olivia," Grandpa Bert said, "always remember that you have a Creator and Sustainer."

"Yes, I read in one of my support magazines, OUR DAILY BREAD, about a man named Phillip who worked with assembling and reassembling the tiny parts of a mechanical watch."

"As he worked with a magnifying glass and tweezers, he meticulously took the watch apart, cleaned it and put the watch back together again. He reassembled the tiny parts of especially mechanical watches. He explained that the essential component of the timepiece was the mainspring."

"The mainspring was the component that moved all the gears to allow the watch to keep time. Without it, even the most expertly designed watch will not function."

"In a beautiful New Testament passage found in the book of Hebrews, the writer eloquently praises Jesus for being the one through whom God created the heavens and the earth. Like the intricacy of a specialty watch, every detail of our universe was created by Jesus Christ, our Lord."

"The Son is Superior to Angels: In the past, God spoke to our forefathers through the prophets at many times and in various ways. But in these last days He has spoken to us by his Son, whom He appointed as heir to all things."

"Through him, he made the universe. The Son is the radiance of God's glory and the exact representation of his being, sustaining all things by His powerful Word. (Hebrews 1;1-4, NIV.)

"Grandma and Grandpa Bert, I don't understand all that you are saying, but I trust you," said Nia Olivia.

"What we are telling you is that you will not have your parents or other family in the same room with you and you will be making your own decisions."

"From the vastness of the solar system to the uniqueness of our fingerprints, all things were made by God. Like a clock or watch's mainspring, Jesus is essential for the function and flourishing of the creation. God's presence continually sustains all things by His powerful word, keeping all that He has created working together in all it's amazing complexity."

"You have many opportunities to experience the beauty of God's creation today. Remember this!"

"He is before all things, and in Him all things hold together." (Colossians 1: 17, NIV.)

"All of us have a calling by God and we have to step out and be a follower of our Creator, recognizing Jesus as the central role in both creating and sustaining the universe. This results in a joyful heart and a response of praise as we acknowledge his ongoing provision for us," I said.

"Little philosophical Kiara said, "I'm happy that Nia Olivia is in college. I'm learning a lot today."

"Nia Olivia and Kiara Janelle, I have laughed many times at my first day of college because my daddy drove my mother and all of my younger siblings and me to the Delaware State University campus. When we entered my dormitory, my whole family had to bring in my stuff," I said.

"Then we went to the president's office instead of the registrar and financial aid office. My father, mother and I went into the president's office. My father gave his money for my tuition to the president. He informed Mr. President that he was placing his daughter, Marian Heath, in his hands."

"A few months later, I received a call from the president of the college, asking me to come and work for him. I also received a music scholarship which was announced at our first choir concert and a letter stating that I had a Delaware State scholarship."

"Apparently Mr. President was impressed with my father and how he handled his business."

I was embarrassed, but Daddy was straight forward. I tremendously enjoyed my college days. It pays to have concerned family members.

"I know from experience that some things that others do will embarrass us. When you are young, you may have issues with our lecturing you, we may say and do things that you do not appreciate."

"Think positive, stay positive, my mother taught me. Don't let someone else rule your mind."

"Be thankful for all gifts. You are unique, beautiful and brilliant." You are creative and make decisions well.

In Philippians, Paul said, "....I have learned to be content whatever the circumstances. I know what it is to be in need, and I know what it is to have plenty. I have learned the secret of being content in any and every situation, whether well fed or hungry, whether living in plenty or in want. I can do everything through Him who gives me strength." (Phil. 4: 12, NIV.)

It's all in God's hand.

CONCLUSION

I AM ALWAYS amazed at the opportunity and privilege of putting words in a book and more fortunate to have others read these words that are put into print. I realize that this whole idea of writing a book is an undertaken not to be taken lightly. It is a challenge as well as a chance and favorable option to hopefully express thoughts that will impress the hearts and minds of other human beings. Thoughts that percolate and become a part of my psyche or subconscious mind continue to give my heart pleasure when I release them on paper. This is an outlet that I have desired for many years. I did not have time to make or take up the issues that I wanted to see come to fruition years past.

As I solemnly engage in the odyssey that brought my family to this point, this milestone in our history, we have fostered the teachings of our ancestors and have reaped the triumphs and achievements which have been inspired by the Word of God and His faithfulness to us. We have the gift that reminds us of the love of family and God.

"One of the most famous orchestral conductors of the twentieth century, Arturo Toscanini, who conducted the New York Philharmonic Orchestra, is always remembered for giving credit where credit is due."

"One author, David Ewen, describes him as being applauded by his orchestral members after a rehearsal of Beethoven's Ninth Symphony. His members rose to their feet and cheered Toscanini at the end of their rehearsal."

"With tears in his eyes, Arturo said "It isn't me. It's Beethoven. Toscanini-nothing! (Paraphrased from Mark Dehaan.)

Paul in the Bible said in essence, "It isn't me, brothers and sisters. It's Christ. Paul is nothing."

"I no longer live, but Christ lives in me." (Galatians 2: 20, NIV.)

I am constantly asked, how do you write, why do you write? As for my writings, I am nothing. God is creating in me, giving me a right spirit.

I see the breaststroke of God's handiwork everywhere, even in darkness.

This book is written for families to understand the significance of names, relationships and dreams. My three Olivias as well as my other grandchildren have a special meaning for me because of the persons who gave them their names. It enhanced my perspective of the persons who gave the names to these children. My children gave my grandchildren the names they have. I appreciate their thoughtfulness and think back on the value placed on those persons who named me.

My mother gave me my first and second names. Marian Anderson was the name of my mother's childhood friend. They were both born in Philadelphia, Pennsylvania and became close friends during my mother's college days in Cheyney State College. Marian Anderson and my mother both had special musical gifts. My mother played the piano for Marian Anderson when they were both unknown.

Marian Anderson became a famous singer; my mother raised many beautiful children and used her talent to enhance children's lives- hers and others.

My second name, Olivia was given to me from another close friend of my Mother.

Names are so important because of the people who name you. Especially is this true because of so many name changes in the black race. Moving from one country to another, denoted many changes including name changes. We know who we are by our name. We know who we are by who names us. We know who we are by whose first name and last name we carry.

Juan Williams points out in his book, MY SOUL LOOKS BACK, "the American idea is unique. Creating one nation out of so many people of different racial and ethnic backgrounds, who speak different languages and have different skin color is an experiment in how these people can stand up to ask for equal opportunities and make their contribution in American life." (p.1.)

"When we look at the entangled structure of the many branches of black family life, and witness one human being such as Barack Obama, first African-American president of the United States, we envision a new world order," states Ellis Cose in his book, THE END OF ANGER.

"Dropping the blinders, reveals how often we heap distain on other people."

"With all its complexities, blacks are optimistic and hopeful for a better future."

"Black hope and white growth are closely related," Cose reiterates. "However, a drastic change in administration can take years away from our strides to upgrade ourselves. Our history evolves from slavery."

"I love to travel throughout this country and other countries with my children and grandchildren. I want them to experience many things and see other people."

I want my children and grandchildren to know that "in Christ was life and in that life we see the light of men. The light shines in the darkness but the darkness has not understood it."

"Know that through Christ all things are possible."

"I am teaching them that they can be just as happy as they set out to be."

They can do all things through Christ because His grace is immeasurable; His peace is inexpressible and His mercy is inexhaustible."

"When it is raining or storming, always look for the rainbow. Look for the light."

"We should try and be that light, as John was. In a world filled with darkness today, people are groping for something to bring light into their darkened lives."

"We can't expect our souls to be comforted without effort on our part."

"Just don't expect to reach our dreams without effort, God is faithful to do his part, but we must do ours." (Blake, p.195.)

"We have seen His glory, the glory of the one and only son, who came from the Father, full of grace and truth." (John 1: 14.)

BIBLIOGRAPHY

Adams, Elaine Parker. THE REVEREND PETER W. CLARK. (Sweet Preacher and Steadfast Reformer), Indiana: Wesbow Press Books, 2013.

Anderson, Joan Wester. GUARDIAN ANGELS. Illinois: Loyola Press, 2006.

Angelou, Maya. LETTERS TO MY DAUGHTERS. New York: Random House, 2008.

.... RAINBOW IN THE CLOUD. New York: Random House, 2014.

.... THE HEART OF A WOMAN. New York: Random House, 1982.

Armour, Vernice. ZERO TO BREAKTHROUGH. New York: Gotham Publishing Co. and Penguin Group, 2011.

Bernard, Emily. BLACK IS THE BODY. New York: Penguin Randon House, LLC., 2019.

Blake, Charles E. FREE TO DREAM. California: Albany Publishing Company, 2000.

Blanco, Richard. FOR ALL OF US, ONE TODAY. New York: Beacon Press, 2013.

Bloomer, George. THROW OFF WHAT HOLDS YOU BACK. Florida: Charisma House, A Strange Company, 2003.

Bollinger, Michele and Dao X. Tran. 101 CHANGEMAKERS: REBELS AND RADICALS WHO CHANGED THE WORLD. Chicago: Haymarket Books, 2012.

Booher, Dianna. SPEAK WITH CONFIDENCE. New York: McGraw-Hill, 2003.

Brandon, Dave, editor. TOGETHER WITH GOD: PSALMS. Michigan: Discovery House, 2016.

Brown, James. ROLE OF A LIFE TIME. New York: Hachatte Book Group, 2009.

Buttworth, Eria. THE CREATIVE LIFE. New York: Penguin Putnam, Inc., 2001.

Carlson, Richard and Kristine. DON'T SWEAT THE SMALL STUFF IN LOVE. New York: 1999.

Cooper, Mariana M. THE AHA FACTOR. London: Wakins Publishing Co., 2016.

Cormer, James P. and Alvin Poussaint. RAISING BLACK CHILDREN. New York: Penguin Group, 1992.

Dowell, Frances. THE AGE OF EMPATHY. New York: Crown Publishing Group, 2014.

Cose, Ellis. THE END OF ANGER. New York: HarperCollins Publishing Co., 2011.

Crowder, Bill. WINDOWS ON CHRISTMAS. Michigan: Discovery House, 2007.

Fredman, Edwin H. GENERATION TO GENERATION. New York: The Guilford Press, 1985.

Habegger, Alfred. MY WARS ARE LAID AWAY IN BOOKS. New York: The Modern Library, 2001.

Hahn, Galen. FINDING MY FIELD. New York: Page Publishing Company, 2018.

Hartley, Leslie. THE GO BETWEEN. London: Hamish Hamilton Co. 1953.

Hughes, Langton. THE NEGRO MOTHER. THE COLLECTED POEMS OF LANGSTON HUGHES. New York: Vintage Classics, 1996.

Hunter, Kristin. GOD BLESS THE CHILD. New York: Scribner Publishing Co. 1964.

Hyatt, Michael. YOUR BEST YEAR EVER. Michigan: Baker Books, 2018.

Jenner, Caitlyn. THE SECRETS OF MY LIFE. New York: Grand Central Publishing, 2017.

Kates, Frederick Ward, BENEATH DAWN AND DARK. The Upper Room. Nashville, Tenn. 1957.

Kerr, Miranda. TREASURE YOURSELF. New York: Hay House, Inc., 2012.

Lee, June N. THE BLACK FAMILY. Michigan: Zondervan Publishing House, 1991.

Leon, Kenny. TAKE YOU WHEREVER YOU GO. New York: Grand Central Publishing Co., 2018.

Linn, Matthew and Linn, Dennis. HEALING THE EIGHT STAGES OF LIFE. New York: Paul's Press, 1988.

Lieberson, S. A PIECE OF THE PIE. Calif: University of California Press, 1980.

Mbugua, Judy. OUR TIME HAS COME. London: The Guerney Press Co. 1994.

McKenley, Rick. THIS BEAUTIFUL MESS. Colorado: Multnomah Books, 2006.

Moore, Darnell L. NO ASHES IN THE FIRE. New York: Nation Books, 2018.

Measom, Chistopher, ed. MICHELLE OBAMA, A PHOGRAPHIC JOURNEY. New York: Sterling Publishing Company, 2017.

Nouwen, Henri. REACHING OUT. New York: Doubleday and company, Inc., 1975.

Obama, Barack. DREAMS OF MY FATHER. New York: Crown Publishing Group, 2004.

--------------------. THE AUDACITY OF HOPE. New York: Crown Publishing Group, 1996.

Obama, Michelle. BECOMING. New York: Crown Publishing Group, 2018.

Rabey, Lois Mowday. WOMEN OF A GENEROUS SPIRIT. Colorado: Waterbrook Press, 1998.

Rainey, Cortez R. FREE YOUR MIND. Create/Space Independent Publishing Platform, 2015.

Robertson, Gil L. FAMILY AFFAIR. Canada: Agate Publishing, Inc. 2009.

Richardson, Cheryl. TAKE TIME FOR YOUR LIFE. New York: Broadway Books, 1998.

Rosanoff, Nancy, Ph.D. KNOWING WHEN IT'S RIGHT. Illinois: Sourcebooks, Inc., 2002.

Russell, A.J. ed. GOD CALLING. Ohio: Barbour Publishing Company, 1993.

Storoni, Mithu. STRESS PROOF. New York: Penguin Random Co., 2017.

Sweeney, M.,Ed. HUGS FROM OBAMA. New York: Castle Point Publishers, LLC., 2018.

Swenson, Kristin M. LIVING THROUGH PAIN. Texas: Baylor University Press, 2005.

Tominey, Shauna. CREATING COMPASSIONATE KIDS. New York: W.W. Norton & Company, 2019.

Trott, James H. A SACRIFICE OF PRAISE. Nashville: Cumberland House Publishing, 1999.

Williams, Juan. MY SOUL LOOKS BACK. New York: HarperCollins Publishing Co., 2003.

Winfrey, Oprah. WHAT I KNOW FOR SURE. Chicago:

Wright, Roosevelt, Jr. TIME TRAVELER TALES. Louisiana: Top Gun Leadership Academy, 2013.

REFERENCE BOOKS

Laird, Charlton. WEBSTER'S NEW ROGET'S A-Z THESAURUS.
  OHIO: Willet Publishing Company,
2003.
RIVERSIDE WEBSTER' NEW COLLEGE DICTIONARY. New
  York: Houghton Mifflin Company, 1995.
THE HOLY BIBLE. THE NEW INTERNATIONAL VERSION.
  Michigan:Vondonvan, 1973.
THE NEW ENCYCLOPEDIA BRITANNICA. Volume 1-24.
  Chicago: Encyclopedia Britannica. First edition, 1768-1771,
  fifteenth ed. 1986.

GATLINBURG, TENNESSEE BROCHURE VACATION GUIDE
GATLINBURG CHAMBER OF COMMERCE
GATLINBURG VISITOR AND CONVENTION CENTER
GATINBURG WELCOME CENTER
GATLINBURG PARKWAY CENTER
GREAT SMOKY MOUNTAINS NATIONAL PARK

On line: www.thejurassicjumbleboatride.com
WONDERWORKS. www.wonderworksonline.com
BEST READ GUIDE. SMOKY MOUNTAINS. Mobi Directory.
  www.brgsm.mobi.
A COMEDY BARN. www.acomedybarn.com.
SOUL OF MOTOWN. www. The grandmajestic co.

SOURCES

www.scouting.org

CPSIA information can be obtained
at www.ICGtesting.com
Printed in the USA
BVHW030838240419
546160BV00034B/152/P